6/he

the SUICIDE

Nicholai Erdman

Adapted & Translated by
Eileen Thalenberg & Alan Richardson

Mosaic Press
"Publishers for Canadian Communities"

Canadian Cataloguing in Publication Data
Erdman, Nikolai
   The suicide
Translation of: Samoubiitsa.
ISBN 0-88962-137-3 (pbk.)

I. Title.
PG3476.E7S213 1981   891.72'44   C81-094604-1

Published by Mosaic Press,
P.O. Box 1032, Oakville, Ontario, Canada, L6J 5E9, 1981

Published with the assistance of the Canada Council and the Ontario Arts Council.

This English translation and adaptation was first performed by Theatre Compact, Toronto, Ontario, Canada, in 1976.

Design by: Doug Frank
Typeset by: Erin Graphics
Printed by: Les Éditions Marquis Ltée
Cover Photo by: Ludvik Dittrick
Cover: Eric House/Barbara Hamilton
      in Theatre Compact's production of The Suicide, 1976

INTRODUCTION

There is relatively little known about the Soviet Dramatist Nikolai Erdman and the biographical information that is available has been the subject of much dispute. Erdman belongs to the generation of writers that fell victim to the prevailing historical and political forces of post-revolutionary Russia; this explains much of the confusion surrounding the details of his life.

Born in 1902, Erdman was not yet 20 when he began writing comedy sketches and satirical material for the theatre. His first play THE MANDATE was produced in 1924 by the Soviet director Meyerhold, known for his daring experiments in the theatre. In 1928 Erdman completed his second play THE SUICIDE. The manuscript attracted the attention of several directors, among them Stanislavski, Meyerhold and Vakhtangov who vied for the right to produce it.

It was Meyerhold who finally won the right to stage THE SUICIDE. But in 1932 (the year that ushered in the second 5 year plan and on the eve of the infamous purges) after 18 months of rehearsal, Stalin's Central Committee attended the dress rehearsal and refused to grant permission for the play to open. To this date THE SUICIDE has never been published or produced in the Soviet Union. It has been translated into several languages and performed in Germany, Switzerland and Yugoslavia. The first English production was in 1976 in the current translation by Theatre Compact in Toronto.

THE SUICIDE is a satire and was considered by many as one of the finest plays in Soviet literature. It falls into the great Russian tradition that embraced the works of Gogol and Sukhovo-Kobylin. The plot revolves around the story of "a little man", Semyon Semyonovich Podsekalnikov who is frustrated and humiliated because he is unemployed. He decided that his only solution is to commit suicide and prepares a suicide note which reads: "In the event of my death, no one is to blame." No sooner does word of his intentions get around, than the whole gamut of Soviet society, including the intelligensia, businessmen, romantic women, invades his home to induce him to die on their behalf and vindicate their particular cause. Although set in Russia in the 1920's, the play has many resonances for the North American audiences of today.

After THE SUICIDE was banned, Erdman disappeared from Moscow. Some say that he was arrested and later sent to Siberia, others say he was only exiled from the capital but lived for many years in poverty. It wasn't until the early 1960's that Erdman's name begins appearing, this time as co-author on a handful of screenplays.

Erdman never wrote for the theatre again. He died in 1970 a stranger to the majority of his own countrymen.

NOTE ON ADAPTATION

In adapting THE SUICIDE we remained faithful to Erdman's original script. Any dramaturgical changes that were made, were done so to reveal the inner intent of the dramatist.

CHARACTERS

SEMYON SEMYONOVICH PODSEKALNIKOV, unemployed
MARIA LUKIANOVNA (MASHA), his wife
SERAFIMA ILYINICHNA, her mother
ALEXANDER PETROVICH KALABUSHKIN, their neighbour
MARGARITA IVANOVNA, his mistress
ARISTARKH DOMINIKOVICH GRAND-SKUBNIK, an intellectual
CLEOPATRA MAXIMOVNA, a romantic
YEGOR TIMOFEEVICH, a Marxist
NIKIFOR PUGACHEV, a butcher
VICTOR VICTOROVICH, a writer
RAISA FILIPOVNA, Cleopatra's rival, a modiste
A YOUNG BOY
A WAITER
A SEAMSTRESS
A DEACON
AN OLD WOMAN

SETTING: Moscow at the end of the 1920's.

the SUICIDE

ACT I

ACT I

A room in SEMYON SEMYONOVICH'S *apartment. Night. The* PODSEKALNIKOVS, SEMYON *and his wife,* MASHA, *are sleeping in a double bed.*

SEMYON	Masha? ...Masha, are you sleeping?
MASHA	*With a start* What?
SEMYON	Ssh, it's just me.
MASHA	Semyon?
SEMYON	Masha, I wanted to ask you ...Masha, are you sleeping?
MASHA	*With a start* What?
SEMYON	Ssh, it's just me.
MASHA	Semyon?
SEMYON	Yes, me.
MASHA	What is it?
SEMYON	Masha...
MASHA	*Rising* Semyon?
SEMYON	Is there any liverwurst left over from dinner?
MASHA	Pardon?
SEMYON	Is there any...
MASHA	Liverwurst?
SEMYON	Left over?
MASHA	Did you look?
SEMYON	I thought...
MASHA	You wake me in the middle of the night...
SEMYON	I'm sorry.
MASHA	...to have a conversation about liverwurst?
SEMYON	No.
MASHA	Your own feet won't carry you?
SEMYON	I thought...
MASHA	That's so insensitive, Semyon.
SEMYON	I...
MASHA	I wouldn't have expected that, Semyon...
SEMYON	I...
MASHA	...even from you — lie down.
SEMYON	I...
MASHA	Down, Semyon, and don't wake me again!
SEMYON	I won't.
MASHA	You won't. *Pause* You know, Semyon, you've destroyed something in me with that liverwurst, yes, destroyed something! I work from six in the morning every day, and when finally I fall into bed exhausted every night, what do

	you do? What do you do, Semyon? Semyon, I'm talking to you! Semyon, are you sleeping?
SEMYON	*With a start* What?
MASHA	Ssh, it's just me.
SEMYON	Masha?
MASHA	I'm talking to you!
SEMYON	What did you say?
MASHA	I said if *you* can't sleep, at least let someone else sleep!
SEMYON	Wait a minute, Masha.
MASHA	No, you wait a minute! Why didn't you eat when it was put in front of you? Mother and I go out of our way to cook your favourite foods...
SEMYON	May I speak too?
MASHA	Why, we put more food on your plate than on anyone else's!
SEMYON	And why do you put more on my plate?
MASHA	Why?!
SEMYON	There's more here than meets the eye!
MASHA	Where? On your plate?
SEMYON	You do it to humiliate...
MASHA	What?!
SEMYON	You want to emphasize the fact in front of everyone...
MASHA	What everyone?
SEMYON	Here sits Semyon Semyonovich, he doesn't work but that doesn't matter, put some more food on his plate!
MASHA	Wait a minute, Semyon.
SEMYON	No, you wait a minute! I have eyes! I'm not as stupid as I may appear!
MASHA	May I speak too?
SEMYON	Your kindness is killing me!
MASHA	That's not true!
SEMYON	And in the middle of the night when I'm lying in bed, starving to death, just the two of us under one blanket and no witnesses, you crucify me!
MASHA	I do?
SEMYON	You deny me my liverwurst!
MASHA	I deny you liverwurst?
SEMYON	In your own way...
MASHA	Eat, Semyon, eat all you like — I'll bring it to you right away! *Masha gets outs of bed, lights a candle. Barefoot with candle in hand, she goes to the door.*
SEMYON	I know what you're doing.
MASHA	God, Semyon, this is a sad way to live. *Exit* *Darkness — Semyon lies in bed.*
SEMYON	I know.

Masha returns to room, in one hand holds the candle, in the other a plate on which there's liverwurst and bread.

MASHA   Semyon, do you want white or black bread with your liverwurst?

SEMYON   The colour of the bread makes no difference to me, I'm not going to eat.

MASHA   Semyon, I'm sorry, I'm tired and sorry if I spoke...

SEMYON   Before, I'd have willingly died from an overdose of liverwurst, but now?

MASHA   Then don't eat!

SEMYON   Do you think that just because I'm unemployed you can order me around!

MASHA   If you're starving, Semyon...

SEMYON   If so, Masha, you'd better think twice, this life is having a terrible effect on me, my heart beats so fast some days. I fear the worst, Masha, I fear, Masha! Here, look what you've done to me!

Semyon sits on the edge of the bed, throws off blanket — hits his knee with the side of his hand, his leg jumps up in reflex action.

Did you see?

MASHA   I saw.

SEMYON   A nervous reaction!

MASHA   Semyon...

SEMYON   A symptom!

Semyon lies down again and pulls the covers up.

MASHA   Maybe you could get a job in a circus with a trick like this, Semyon, but it's no way to live.

SEMYON   No way to live?

MASHA   That's what I said.

SEMYON   Then what do you suggest?

MASHA   I...

SEMYON   In your opinion, what should I do? Masha, what do you want?

MASHA   I...

SEMYON   My dying breath? Is that it? — my corpse! You'll get it, Masha, I swear! Is that what you want? Eh? You'll get it, Masha.

MASHA   Don't get excited, Semyon.

SEMYON   I wouldn't disappoint you in this, oh no, and I'll tell you why, Masha — I'll let you in on a little secret, Masha... You disgust me!

MASHA   What?!

SEMYON   On principle I won't say another word — except to add you're a bitch!

	The candlestick falls from Masha's hand and breaks. The room is completely dark again. Pause.
	Enter Serafima, standing in doorway.
SERAFIMA	Masha, you know I never intrude, but perhaps you could explain to me why things are falling on your floor in the middle of the night? You'll wake everyone in the building! Masha? Masha, why don't you say something?
MASHA	On principle.
SERAFIMA	What principle?
MASHA	Ask Semyon.
SERAFIMA	Semyon, what's happening? — Semyon?
MASHA	Semyon?
SERAFIMA	Speak!
MASHA	Semyon?
SERAFIMA	Are you a stone?
MASHA	Have you had a stroke?
SERAFIMA	A stroke!
MASHA	Semyon?
SERAFIMA	Oh Merciful God!
MASHA	I'll look, Mother.
	In the dark Masha's cautious steps can be heard.
	Semyon? Semyon? *Pause* Mother!
SERAFIMA	What!
MASHA	Light the candle!
SERAFIMA	Where...
MASHA	On the floor!
SERAFIMA	On the floor.
MASHA	Semyon, darling, don't frighten me — Semyon, please... *Pause* Mother!
SERAFIMA	What?
MASHA	Hurry!
SERAFIMA	I'm on the floor.
MASHA	Try over by the door!
SERAFIMA	Try over by the door.
MASHA	Semyon, I can't stand any more!
	A loud thump and Serafima's 'OW!'
	Mother of God, what was that!
SERAFIMA	The door, Masha, my head and the door.
MASHA	Try over by the chair!
SERAFIMA	Try over by the chair.
MASHA	Semyon, it's not amusing to torture me like this! It's not fair!
	A crash, Serafima's 'OW!'
	Holy Mother!
SERAFIMA	I found it, Masha!

4

MASHA	Hurry!
SERAFIMA	*Striking match* There!
MASHA	Something dreadful has happened, Mother.
SERAFIMA	Poor Semyon.
MASHA	*Throws back blanket* Look!
SERAFIMA	Semyon?
MASHA	Gone!
SERAFIMA	And his stroke...
MASHA	He's gone. *Runs around the room* Semyon!
SERAFIMA	*Going to Masha* That's peculiar.
MASHA	*Runs to bed* The candle! Bring the candle over here! *Masha snatches it from Serafima, places it on the floor, gets down on her knees and looks under the bed.*
SERAFIMA	Of course he always was!
MASHA	Oh, my God, right against the wall! *Masha crawls under bed*
SERAFIMA	Semyon Semyonovich, this is no way to behave! Masha, come back, leave him there! A sulk is one thing, but this...
MASHA	*Crawling out from under the bed holding her shoes* Here they are — I'm going outside, Mother.
SERAFIMA	Semyon?
MASHA	Hand me my skirt, Mother. *Serafima runs to dresser.* The candle, leave the candle! *Serafima runs back to bed.* I'll get it myself! *Masha runs to wall and pulls a bunch of clothes off peg*
SERAFIMA	Where are you going?
MASHA	*At bed, finds skirt* I must bring him back, Mother, he's in no condition to be otside — he even showed me his symptom in bed...
SERAFIMA	His what?
MASHA	And I didn't believe him!
SERAFIMA	And what exactly did *you* do, Masha?
MASHA	Mother!
SERAFIMA	Yes?
MASHA	What if *he* does something to himself?
SERAFIMA	As the Good Lord said, Masha, in a proper marriage...
MASHA	*Rummaging among clothes* My blouse, where's my blouse?
SERAFIMA	Praise be to God! His pants.
MASHA	His pants?
SERAFIMA	If his pants are here, it means he's here!
MASHA	*Putting on blouse* Mother, he was in such a state...
SERAFIMA	A civilized man without pants is like a man without eyes, he can't go anywhere — then again, in Semyon's case...
MASHA	Then where is he, Mother?
SERAFIMA	Try the bathroom!

MASHA	The bathroom? *She runs off* Of course!
SERAFIMA	That our family should come to this!
MASHA	*Re-entering* Mother, what will I say?
SERAFIMA	Say?
MASHA	When he hears my voice, what if he...
SERAFIMA	*Going to icon* Pray, Masha.
MASHA	You remember the Chertkovs...
SERAFIMA	I remember — one shot, one head of family gone, literally.
MASHA	It's horrible! — but I must! *Going*
SERAFIMA	*Kneeling* The Lord helps them that...
MASHA	I can't help myself! *Exit*
	Serafima, alone, praying at the icon
SERAFIMA	Blessed mothers of Uutivan, of Vatapad, of Kupiatist, of Novo-nikito, or Arapet, of Pskov, of Vydropus, of Smolensk, of Sviatogorsk, of Vienna, of Svienna, of Ibersk, of Abalata-Znamenie, of Bratsk, of Kiev, of Pimenov of Spain, and of Kazan — all of you pray to your son for the good health of my son-in-law. Blessed Virgin, open the door of mercy to us.
	Enter Masha, running
MASHA	The door is latched and won't open.
SERAFIMA	Did you talk to him?
MASHA	In a way...
SERAFIMA	What did he say?
MASHA	Nothing — he refuses to answer.
SERAFIMA	What next!
MASHA	I'll wake up Alexander Petrovich!
SERAFIMA	You mustn't!
MASHA	*Going* He can break the door down.
SERAFIMA	Wait! — He buried his wife last week.
MASHA	That means he'll understand the meaning of compassion!
	Masha runs to Alexander's door
SERAFIMA	Compassion doesn't knock down doors, Masha!
MASHA	He can, Mother! *Pounds on door* Alexander Petrovich!
SERAFIMA	My God, everyone in the building will hear!
MASHA	Mother, go and listen at the bathroom door, maybe Semyon's started moving around!
	Pounds on door. Serafima exits
	Alexander Petrovich.
ALEXANDER	*Behind door* Who's there?
MASHA	Comrade, it's me!
ALEXANDER	Who?
MASHA	Masha! I need you!
ALEXANDER	Need me?

6

MASHA	Comrade, you must help me!
ALEXANDER	Be quiet!
MASHA	I'm only a woman, what can I do!
ALEXANDER	Take a cold shower, Masha!
MASHA	*Pounds on door* I have to break the door down!
ALEXANDER	For God's sake, don't! Stop!
	Doors open, Margarita appears in door
MARGARITA	Break the door down? An interesting pastime for a young lady! Oh, pardon me, did I say young lady? I meant tramp!
MASHA	Tramp?
MARGARITA	Alexander Petrovich and I were just sitting here in deep mourning...
MASHA	Alexander Petrovich and I are...
MARGARITA	Obviously! — but in a time of mourning...
MASHA	Alexander Petrovich is a strong man...
MARGARITA	...Have you no respect for the deceased?
MASHA	...The respected owner of a shooting gallery...
MARGARITA	Obviously not, since at a time like this...
MASHA	Why won't you listen to me!
MARGARITA	You want to break the door down.
MASHA	But it wasn't this door I wanted to break down!
MARGARITA	There are others? — as I said...
MASHA	Please listen.
MARGARITA	A tramp!
ALEXANDER	*Sticking head out* Margarita, if you are going to hit her, I advise against it...
MASHA	Alexander Petrovich! *Alexander withdraws head quickly*
MARGARITA	Must I speak plainly?
ALEXANDER	*Behind door* You're not registered in this building.
MARGARITA	Why are you chasing someone else's husband?
MASHA	You've misunderstood, I'm a married woman!
MARGARITA	No misunderstanding, I'm married myself!
MASHA	But my husband is shooting himself!
	Alexander charges out of room. Margarita knocks into Masha, both go down
ALEXANDER	Semyon? Where?
MASHA	In the bathroom!
ALEXANDER	*Charging off* Why didn't you say so!
MARGARITA	Why is your husband shooting himself in the bathroom?
MASHA	Where else can an unemployed man go!
	Re-enter Alexander
ALEXANDER	He has a gun, you say? We must be careful in that case.
MASHA	If he fires when we start...
MARGARITA	You can't break the door down!
ALEXANDER	*To Masha* In that case we'll be very careful.

7

MARGARITA	Send for the police.
ALEXANDER &	
MASHA	No!
ALEXANDER	We'll sneak up on the door and then you say something gentle to him and then I — *makes a gesture of charging the door* — but quietly.
MASHA	God will bless you, Alexander Petrovich!
MARGARITA	Ridiculous!
ALEXANDER	You flatter me! Now, quietly... like this... on tiptoes.
	Alexander and Masha tiptoe across stage; after hesitation, Margarita joins them
	Ssh...
MARGARITA	The police...
ALEXANDER &	
MASHA	Ssh...
	A cry is heard offstage — all three recoil. Alexander runs to his room and closes the door. Masha and Margarita collide, go down
	Enter Serafima, running
SERAFIMA	Don't go in there!
MASHA	My God, it happened!
ALEXANDER	*Opening door* What happened?
SERAFIMA	It wasn't Semyon, it was Volodkina's grandmother from the other wing!
MASHA	What?
SERAFIMA	I saw her with my own eyes, she just came out and I was standing there like an idiot, listening at the door... *she spits* Phoo...
ALEXANDER	There seems to be some mistake, Masha.
MASHA	It's your fault, Mother.
SERAFIMA	My fault! Did you hear!
MARGARITA	Don't look at me!
ALEXANDER	It's not mine.
SERAFIMA	My fault!
MASHA	I told you he was outside!
MARGARITA	Send for the police.
MASHA	I beg you, Alexander Petrovich...
SERAFIMA	*To Margarita* Who are you?
MASHA	... on my knees.
MARGARITA	*To Serafima* Who are you?
MASHA	Help me look outside on the street.
SERAFIMA	How can he be outside without his pants?
MARGARITA	Without...?
ALEXANDER	Did you search the entire house?
SERAFIMA	*To Margarita* This used to be a quiet building.

MASHA	Everywhere.
SERAFIMA	Not in the kitchen.
MASHA	Not in the kitchen! *She runs for exit*
ALEXANDER	Not in the kitchen! *He runs for exit*
MARGARITA	Not in the kitchen? *She walks for exit*
SERAFIMA	Not in the kitchen.
ALEXANDER	*At exit* You stay here, Margarita! *Exits after Masha*
MARGARITA	Stay here? *Going to exit* I don't trust you two...
SERAFIMA	Wait!
MARGARITA	Why?
SERAFIMA	Do I know you?
MARGARITA	*Going* Oh, for God's sake...
SERAFIMA	Stop!
	At that moment we hear: 'Alex, stop!,' the slamming of a door, an inhuman screech from Semyon and finally the sound of a body falling to the floor, followed by complete silence
MARGARITA	We'll stay here.
SERAFIMA	He shot himself, the party's over.
MARGARITA	I thought the revolution was over!
SERAFIMA	Suicide! — how can I pray?
MARGARITA	Who's in charge here?
SERAFIMA	That it should happen to us!
MARGARITA	Why is it always me?
SERAFIMA	I'm going to scream!
MARGARITA	Who witnesses these gruesome events!
SERAFIMA	Do something desperate myself!
MARGARITA	Stop it! Be calm like me.
SERAFIMA	What are we going to do!
MARGARITA	What's the matter with you!
	Door is kicked open. Both Margarita and Sarafima scream and run for icon. Alexander enters dragging Semyon
SEMYON	I repeat, what's the matter with you?
ALEXANDER	Don't get upset, Semyon Semyonovich.
SEMYON	Where are you dragging me?
ALEXANDER	I'm your friend, Semyon Semyonovich.
SEMYON	Let go! Let go of me!
SERAFIMA	*Grabbing Semyon* Don't let go of him!
MARGARITA	*Grabbing Semyon* Hold on, hold on to him!
ALEXANDER	We're all your friends, Semyon Semonovich!
SERAFIMA	Where's Masha?
ALEXANDER	Lying on the kitchen floor.
MARGARITA	Lying?
ALEXANDER	Fainted.
SERAFIMA	On the floor!

ALEXANDER	Out cold.
SERAFIMA	*Running off* Holy Mother, what'll happen next? *Exit*
MARGARITA	*Walking off* I'll handle this. *Exit*
SEMYON	Excuse me, Alexander Petrovich, but may I ask why you have your hand in my pocket?
ALEXANDER	Give it to me!
SEMYON	Give what to you?
ALEXANDER	I saw you putting it in your mouth.
SEMYON	Alexander Petrovich, are you well? Let go, let go of me!
ALEXANDER	I will... but first give me your word, Semyon Semyonovich, that you won't try anything until you've heard me out, I beg you, as a friend, just hear me out.
SEMYON	I'm listening.
ALEXANDER	*Releasing him* Thank you.
SEMYON	*To himself* Thank God.
ALEXANDER	*Pulling Semyon down* Please sit down.
SEMYON	Thank you.
	Alexander strikes a pose in front of Semyon
ALEXANDER	Comrade Podsekalnikov...
SEMYON	Yes?
ALEXANDER	One moment...
	Alexander runs to window, a depressing morning lights up the messy bed, the overturned furniture and the joyless state of the room
	Comrade Podsekalnikov... life is beautiful.
SEMYON	What does that have to do with me?
ALEXANDER	What does it have to do with you? Comrade, where have you been? This is the twentieth century. The age of enlightenment. The age of electricity.
SEMYON	And what kind of age is it when the electricity is turned off because of an unpaid bill?
ALEXANDER	Good question, Comrade.
SEMYON	The Stone Age?
ALEXANDER	It's like living in caves, isn't it? I spent three weeks standing in queues just to get my bill adjusted, their error of course — but that's beside the point, that's always beside the point, whatever the case it's always your fault, and you ask yourself finally, do I live just for that? NO! You get tired of living just for that!
SEMYON	Isn't it the truth.
ALEXANDER	Just plain tired of living! — what am I saying? You're confusing me, Semyon Semyonovich! — where was I?
SEMYON	The age of enlightenment.
ALEXANDER	Comrade Podsekalnikov... life is beautiful.
SEMYON	I read that in Pravda too, but I think they will retract it soon.

ALEXANDER	There's your problem, you think too much.
SEMYON	I do?
ALEXANDER	Look at Fedya Petunin, there's an example for you — a model citizen, won an award for best worker in his factory, assembly line number six, nuts and bolts — mark my words, Comrade Podsekalnikov, in his example lies your answer.
SEMYON	What was the question?
ALEXANDER	When he works, he works, he doesn't think.
SEMYON	You're not allowed to work if you're unemployed.
ALEXANDER	You're still waiting for your clearance papers? *Semyon nods his head 'yes.'* You stand in line? *Semyon nods his head 'yes.'* What a system! Ah, life's a struggle, Semyon Semyonovich.
SEMYON	And who said I didn't struggle?
ALEXANDER	I didn't.
SEMYON	I admit at times I'm not the happiest of men...
ALEXANDER	But a man needs a vocation.
SEMYON	...but I try, my temper sometimes...
ALEXANDER	We need a purpose in our lives.
SEMYON	And who said I didn't have a purpose?
ALEXANDER	I didn't, farthest thing from my mind!
SEMYON	Look at this. *Taking out book*
ALEXANDER	What is it?
SEMYON	A manual for playing the tuba.
ALEXANDER	The tuba.
SEMYON	You can learn in only twenty lessons. There's a gold mine in it. *Shows pile of papers from under pillow* Approximately twenty concerts a month at five and a half rubles a piece, that comes to: 1,320 rubles — clear. So, as you can see, Alexander Petrovich, everything is ready — I have the desire, the manual, I've made my calculations, the only thing missing is the tuba.
ALEXANDER	That's a common fate, Comrade, but what can you do? Life must go on.
SEMYON	It certainly must.
ALEXANDER	You agree?
SEMYON	I agree.
ALEXANDER	That means I've convinced you. Thank you! Thank God! Hand over the gun.
SEMYON	What gun?
ALEXANDER	I saw you put it in your mouth.
SEMYON	Not again.
ALEXANDER	Are you trying to make a fool out of me?
SEMYON	Me?
ALEXANDER	Everyone knows *you* were committing suicide!

SEMYON	I was?
ALEXANDER	You were!
SEMYON	Why would I?
ALEXANDER	You don't know?
SEMYON	I'm asking you!
ALEXANDER	Because it's been a year since you worked anywhere and you're ashamed of living off other people.
SEMYON	That's true — who said that!?
ALEXANDER	I didn't, don't get upset.
SEMYON	It was Masha, wasn't it?
ALEXANDER	Well, I have to admit...
SEMYON	Oh God, I knew it — get out of here!
ALEXANDER	First hand over the gun, then I'll go.
SEMYON	Look, it can't be so difficult to understand, I have no gun! Where would I get a gun?
ALEXANDER	It's not difficult these days — Panfidich traded his razor for one down at Borzov's on Market Street.
SEMYON	For a razor?
ALEXANDER	And you're going to hand yours over for nothing! You haven't a permit, and if the police find out — bang, six months hard labour! Hand it over!
SEMYON	I can't.
ALEXANDER	Then, forgive me, but you've only yourself to blame. I'll have to use force. *He grabs Semyon*
SEMYON	Alexander Petrovich, I'll let you in on a little secret — if you don't get out of here immediately, I'll shoot myself before your very eyes.
ALEXANDER	You wouldn't.
SEMYON	You don't believe me? Fine, I'll count to three. One...
ALEXANDER	Yes, he would.
SEMYON	Two...
ALEXANDER	I'm gone! *Like a bullet into his room*
SEMYON	Three... *He takes a roll of sausage out of his pocket; takes a bite* Where's the plate? *Puts sausage on plate* There. She'll never guess I ate any at all — Well, Masha, I'm a burden, am I? I'll teach you a lesson. *Runs to table and begins to rummage around* I'll show you what it feels like to be dependent on you. Just wait! *Finds razor* Swedish steel, my father's! ...to hell with it, I may not be shaving in this world any more! *Running off* Borzov's on Market Street... *Exit Alexander re-enters*
ALEXANDER	*To himself* Am I afraid of idle threats? *Kitchen door is kicked open* I'm going! *Serafima enters dragging an unconscious Masha, followed by Margarita*

SERAFIMA	Careful — careful — Alexander Petrovich!
MARGARITA	Don't drag her on the floor.
ALEXANDER	Careful, careful.
SERAFIMA	Holy Mother...
MARGARITA	*To Alexander* Stand back, give her room to breathe!
SERAFIMA	Preserve us from our friends!
ALEXANDER	I'll undo her buttons.
MASHA	Who's there?
SERAFIMA	Masha!
ALEXANDER	Don't be embarassed...
MASHA	Did he die? What happened?
ALEXANDER	No, he hasn't died, Masha, but I must be honest with you, he's planning to.
MASHA	We must stop him!
ALEXANDER	Don't even try.
SERAFIMA	Why?
ALEXANDER	He said to me, 'if you do not leave this room at once I will shoot myself before your very eyes.'
MASHA	And what did you do?
ALEXANDER	I tried a little of this, a little of that, I pleaded, I begged him, but nothing worked.
SERAFIMA	You left.
MARGARITA	You have to order, not beg! Call the police, they'll arrest him and bring him to trial.
ALEXANDER	Alas, there's no such law.
SERAFIMA	The law can't sentence a man to life.
MARGARITA	Nonsense!
ALEXANDER	To death yes, but not to life.
SERAFIMA	*To Margarita* Who are you?
MASHA	Then what can we do?!
MARGARITA	Do? It's obvious, I repeat...
MASHA	No!
ALEXANDER	Indeed it is obvious...
SERAFIMA	We say no!
MASHA	It's up to us, Mother.
SERAFIMA	He'll come home...
MASHA	We must do something...
ALEXANDER	Ladies?
MASHA	Or I'll go crazy!
SERAFIMA	When he's hungry.
ALEXANDER	Ladies?
SERAFIMA	Then I'll break both his legs!
MASHA	We're his only salvation!
ALEXANDER	His salvation is a tuba!
MASHA	A tuba?

SERAFIMA	A what?
MASHA	*Beginning to laugh* What next!?
SERAFIMA	Why?
MASHA	*Laughing* A tuba!
ALEXANDER	To earn money — if he gets a tuba I can guarantee he won't shoot himself.
MASHA	*Laughing* A tuba...
SERAFIMA	How much does one cost?
ALEXANDER	Five hundred rubles.
MASHA	Five hundred rubles?
SERAFIMA	If we ever have five hundred rubles I can guarantee he won't shoot himself with or without a tuba!
ALEXANDER	That's true.
MASHA	My God, I'll die laughing!
MARGARITA	I have a tuba.
MASHA	Of course you do.
SERAFIMA	You do?
MASHA	Why wouldn't you!
MARGARITA	*To Masha* Listen, dearie...
ALEXANDER	She has an entire symphony orchestra at her restaurant!
MASHA	*Laughing* Wonderful!
SERAFIMA	How many tubas?
MARGARITA	At least five.
MASHA	Five tubas!
SERAFIMA	You're both crazy!
MARGARITA	*To Alexander* Disgusting friends you have!
MASHA	Mother, the world's upside down!
SERAFIMA	Masha, calm down.
ALEXANDER	Ladies, allow me to introduce...
MASHA	Everyone has a tuba!
MARGARITA	*To Alexander* No names!
MASHA	But us!
MARGARITA	If my husband were to find out!
ALEXANDER	My dear friend and comfort...
SERAFIMA	Shut up! — Masha...
ALEXANDER	Margarita Ivanovna, what can I do?
SERAFIMA	Margarita Ivanovna?
MARGARITA	*To Alexander* Be quiet!
SERAFIMA	That Margarita Ivanovna?
MASHA	*To Serafima* The one with the restaurant?
MARGARITA	I'm as good as dead.
SERAFIMA	*To Masha* The one with the orchestra.
ALEXANDER	Ladies, I've made a mistake, this is not...
MASHA	Your tuba...
MARGARITA	*Sweetly* Yes?

SERAFIMA	We'd do anything!
MARGARITA	Well, my musicians...
MASHA	Anything.
ALEXANDER	Perhaps a small rental fee...
MARGARITA	Well, there is something...
MASHA	Thank God! Talk to them!
SERAFIMA	There's no time to lose!
MASHA	I'll help you get ready and go with you.
MARGARITA	*Starting to go with Masha* Husbands are a great trial always!
ALEXANDER	*Following* I still think a small fee...
SERAFIMA	We're saved! The Lord works in mysterious ways!
MARGARITA	We're going to be friends, don't you feel? *Exit*
SERAFIMA	We're not — Alexander Petrovich, wait!
ALEXANDER	What is it?
SERAFIMA	What if he... before the tuba comes?
ALEXANDER	Distract him.
SERAFIMA	Wait! — how?
ALEXANDER	I suggest, Serafima, that you brazenly walk into his room, pretending you know nothing and start telling him stories.
SERAFIMA	Me?
ALEXANDER	Use your sense of humour.
SERAFIMA	Mine?
ALEXANDER	And tell him funny stories.
SERAFIMA	I don't know any.
ALEXANDER	Oh, I don't know, make up something, your son-in-law's life's at stake — it's no laughing matter. *He exits*
SERAFIMA	*Alone* My God, what am I going to tell him? *Exit* *Enter Semyon, looks around uneasily. Takes a gun out of his pocket. Sits down at table, opens inkwell, tears off sheet of paper*
SEMYON	*Writing* In the event of my death... *Serafima re-enters*
SERAFIMA	Oh, God!
SEMYON	Pardon?
SERAFIMA	*To herself* Sense of humour — Good morning, Semyon Semyonovich. I have something to tell you, you'll die laughing! Excuse me...
SEMYON	Serafima?
SERAFIMA	Did you ever hear the one about the Germans?
SEMYON	No.
SERAFIMA	These Germans ate a Bowser alive.
SEMYON	Which Germans?
SERAFIMA	I don't remember which ones, they just ate it! My late husband used to tell this one just after the war, did we ever laugh! *Pause* A Bowser is a dog, Semyon Semyonovich.

SEMYON	So?
SERAFIMA	People don't eat dogs alive.
SEMYON	So?
SERAFIMA	So they ate it.
SEMYON	So?
SERAFIMA	Where's your sense of humour?
SEMYON	Serafima...
SERAFIMA	Here's another one in the same vein.
SEMYON	Would you please leave.
SERAFIMA	Picture this! — during the war in our village we had a Turkish prisoner in jail — anyhow, he was shell shocked and his head used to shake all the time like this. It was hilarious — so what do you think happened?
SEMYON	Serafima, can't you see I'm busy?
SERAFIMA	They decided one evening...
SEMYON	I'm begging you!
SERAFIMA	One evening they took him some bread and meat and said to him 'do you want something to eat?' Now this Turk is dying for food but he can't speak Russian so he jumps up and his head is shaking like this — well the crowd had expected that and took all the food back — 'You don't want, you don't want!' Did we ever laugh about that Turk! Well?
SEMYON	Get the hell out of here!
SERAFIMA	What's the matter, Semyon Semyonovich? There was this other one...
	Semyon has grabbed pen, paper and inkwell and is running for the exit
SERAFIMA	Stop! Where are you going? Alexander the Great squashed this Jew against the Palace Gate...
	Exit Semyon. Serafima, alone at door
	No sense of humour — I'll just have to keep trying!
	Heaving on door — it opens.
	Let me in! *Exit. Enter Alexander, Masha and Margarita*
ALEXANDER	Hurry, Margarita!
MASHA	Where's Semyon now?
ALEXANDER	With your Mother — I told her what to do!
	All three exit. Semyon jumps out from door
SEMYON	*Screaming at door* If you tell me one more stupid story about a Bowser, I'll eat you alive! *Slams door shut* And don't follow me around, you old idiot!
	Having locked the door, Semyon goes to table.
	Reading In the event of my death... *Writing* no one is to blame, signed, Semyon Semyonovich Podsekalnikov.
	Semyon looks at gun, eats sausage again
	CURTAIN

END OF ACT ONE

the *SUICIDE*

ACT II

ACT II	*Same room as in Act I — everything has been put in order. Semyon is seated on a stool with an enormous tuba strapped to his shoulder. The manual is open in front of him. Masha and Serafima to the side on chairs.*
SEMYON	*Reading* 'Chapter I, titled, How to Play. To play the tuba a combination of three fingers is used. The first finger goes on the first valve, the second on the second valve, the third on the third valve...' like this... 'upon blowing into the mouthpiece the note B is obtained...' *Blows, blows again* What's this? All air, no sound.
SERAFIMA	Hold your breath, Masha, if he gets disillusioned we're lost.
SEMYON	Wait! Wait!! Here's a separate chapter... 'How to Blow... In order to blow properly I — the internationally renowned sound artist Theordor Hugo Schultz — suggest a simple and economical method. Tear off a little piece of yesterday's newspaper and place it on the tongue.'
SERAFIMA	On the tongue?
SEMYON	On the tongue? Serafima, hand me yesterday's Pravda.
SERAFIMA	*Running to get the paper* Yesterday's Pravda?
SEMYON	Tear off a piece.
MASHA	A smaller piece, Mother, smaller.
SEMYON	Now place it on my tongue. *She does so*
SERAFIMA	Now what?
SEMYON	.... *Unintelligible mumbling*
SERAFIMA	What?
SEMYON	*More mumbling*
SERAFIMA	I don't understand.
SEMYON	*Spits out paper* STUPID! I said, understand now? I asked you simply to **read on**... 'Tear off a little piece of yesterday's newspaper and place it on the tongue'... then what?
MASHA	*Running to book* And then, Semyon, it says... *reads* 'Spit the piece of paper onto the floor.'
SERAFIMA	Of course.
MASHA	'While spitting, try to memorize the position of your mouth. Having mastered this position, blow just like you spit'... that's all.
SERAFIMA	How else would you blow a tuba?
SEMYON	Silence! Attention please... *tears off piece of paper* Move over to one side, Serafima... *Places it and spits, blows in mouthpiece*

	Hell, not a sound.
SERAFIMA	The party's over, he's getting discouraged.
	Semyon spits again and prepares to blow
MASHA	Dear God, if you exist, send him a sound!
	At that moment the room is filled with the bellow of the tuba
SERAFIMA	Living proof!
SEMYON	Masha, your working days are over.
MASHA	Over?
SERAFIMA	What'll we live on?
SEMYON	I have it all worked out. Approximately twenty concerts a month times five and a half rubles, in a year that works out to... one moment *looking through pockets* I have it somewhere here *takes out slip of paper and reads* 'In the event of my...' *Pause* wrong paper *hides it and takes out another* Here, here it is. In one year my earnings will be 1,320 rubles. There! And you ask what will we live on!
SERAFIMA	But you haven't learned how to play yet.
SEMYON	Did I spit?
MASHA	Mother.
SEMYON	For me to learn, Serafima, is as easy as spitting.
	Takes a piece of paper. Spits. Blows. Tuba bellows.
	Did you hear? With this tuba, Serafima, the world's our oyster. Again? *Taking piece of paper*
MASHA	It's wonderful, Semyon!
SEMYON	*Paper on tongue* It is! It is! Masha, just think how wonderful! ...to come home after a concert with a good paycheck, to sit down on a sofa surrounded by your family and relax...
SERAFIMA	Good Lord!
SEMYON	Were the painters here today? And you answer, Masha, Yes, dear, the nursery is all ready.
	Semyon and Masha join hands
SERAFIMA	The nursery!
SEMYON	And the new drapes we picked out, did they arrive?
MASHA	Yes, dear Semyon.
SEMYON	Good, I was worried about those — well, let's have some eggnog.
SERAFIMA	Eggnog!
SEMYON	By the way, from now on I will have eggnog with all my meals, in the first place it's good for the chest — and in the second place, I like eggnog.
MASHA	But Semyon, eggs are very expensive.
SEMYON	Expensive? Who's bringing in the money now, you or me?
SERAFIMA	Learn how to play first, and then...

SEMYON	Why do you always argue with me, Serafima, why don't you just keep quiet and listen to the music. *Blows*
MASHA	Wonderful.
SEMYON	I would like to request the appropriate silence during these moments of creativity... *reads* 'Scales. The scale is the umbilical cord of music. Once you master the umbilical cord, you are re-born as a musician...' well, now I'll master it... *Reads*
MASHA	Perhaps we will have a nursery, Mother, why shouldn't we?
SEMYON	*Reading* '...in order to properly learn a scale I — the internationally renowned artist of sound Theodor Hugo Schultz — suggest the most inexpensive method. Go out an buy the cheapest pi... *Turns page* ...ano'. Piano?
SERAFIMA & MASHA	Piano?
SEMYON	Wait a minute, that's impossible! *Reads* 'I suggest the most inexpensive method. Go out and but the cheapest pi... *Checks to see if pages are stuck together* ...ano'. Why would I need a piano?
SERAFIMA	Read on.
MASHA	Read on, Semyon.
SEMYON	*Reads* 'In the footnotes you will find the explanation of why you need a piano...'
MASHA	The footnote, there.
SEMYON	'play the scale first on the piano, then repeat it on the tuba'.
SERAFIMA	What does this mean?
MASHA	There's some mistake!
SEMYON	It means you're a son of a bitch!
MASHA	Semyon!
SEMYON	An artist of sound! Ha! You're no artist, Theordor Hugo Schultz! You're a bastard! You and your umbilical cord! *Tearing up manual*
SERAFIMA	You can't trust anyone these days.
SEMYON	Masha, how can I buy a piano? What has he done to me! *Holding up pieces of manual* I looked to you as my rock of salvation, my entire future depended on this tuba!
MASHA	Calm down, Semyon.
SEMYON	How will we live!
MASHA	I can still work, Semyon.
SERAFIMA	We've gotten by on Masha's salary till now...
SEMYON	Oh, have we!?
SERAFIMA	We'll manage again.
SEMYON	Meaning I don't count?!
SERAFIMA	If dreams were rubles...
SEMYON	You're forgetting one thing, Serafima — as far as I'm

	concerned Masha's salary is only supplementary income. This place was completely furnished when she moved in! Who bought these saucers, Serafima? I did! And when these saucers get broken, will you have enough money to buy new ones?
MASHA	Don't worry, Semyon, we'll have enough.
SEMYON	Enough?
MASHA	Enough.
SEMYON	*Throws saucer on floor* Well now, we'll see... and when these cups get broken, will you have enough to buy new ones?
MASHA	No! There won't be enough.
SEMYON	You see? We can't go on living like this. All that's left is for me to... get out of here! Both of you! Three of us can't live on one salary!
MASHA	God have mercy on you, and on us, Semyon, there will be enough money for you!
SEMYON	How can there be enough for me when there's not enough for cups?
MASHA	There will be enough, Semyon — Mother!
SERAFIMA	There will be enough.
SEMYON	Enough. *Drops cup* And when this vase breaks, Masha, will you have enough to buy a new one?
SERAFIMA	Say there won't be enough.
MASHA	There won't be enough!
SEMYON	Then get out of here!
MASHA	I've had enough!
SERAFIMA	That makes two of us.
MASHA	You'll have to kill me first, I'm not leaving.
SEMYON	Not leaving?
MASHA	Not leaving.
SEMYON	Well now, we'll see. *Drops vase*
MASHA	Are you planning to break everything, Semyon?
SEMYON	Yes, everything.
MASHA	Well now, we'll see. *Smashes mirror*
SEMYON	You... how dare you? In front of me...? In front of the head of the...? Oh my God! Leave me alone, I beg you, if you've any kindness left, leave me, please, leave me alone! *Masha marches out, Serafima follows. Semyon locks the door behind them* Our beautiful mirror, a wedding present, broken... everything's broken, cups, saucers, life — how could she? — broken... and no one gives a damn! Not the world, the universe, humanity — they take your coffin and shove it under and only two people, if two, care what remains, that's

all there is to humanity! How many people do I know? I pass people on the street every day, hundreds, thousands, what difference does it make? They mean nothing to me, it makes no sense... two, if two, will follow what remains, my remains, if I remain... broken. We'll manage.

Takes note out of pocket

Or maybe we won't. *Jumps up* No, we won't!

Puts revolver to head

Here's eggnog for you, Semyon Semyonovich!

At this moment a deafening knock at the door. Semyon hides gun behind his back

My God. Who's there?

Door flies open and in walks Aristarkh Dominikovich Grand-Skubnik

ARISTARKH	Pardon me, did I interrupt? If you were in the middle of something, please continue.
SEMYON	No, no, I'm in no hurry, actually... what can I do for you?
ARISTARKH	First of all, may I know to whom I am speaking?
SEMYON	*After pause* Podsekalnikov, I think, I'm sure, yes.
ARISTARKH	My pleasure — allow me to inquire, are you not the same Podsekalnikov who is committing suicide?
SEMYON	Who said so? I mean no. *Aside* Now they'll arrest me for possession of a firearm — No, I'm not, I'm not the one, I swear to God.
ARISTARKH	How is that possible? Here's the address, and... *Sees note on table* and here? *Picking it up* 'In the event of my death no one is to blame,' and signed...
SEMYON	Podsekalnikov.
ARISTARKH	Yes.
SEMYON	Yes. *Aside* I'm dead.
ARISTARKH	Look here, comrade, that's no way to act.
SEMYON	I was thinking that too.
ARISTARKH	It's based on the wrong point of view.
SEMYON	Pardon?
ARISTARKH	What good would it do not to blame anyone? On the contrary you should accuse and blame. You are shooting yourself, that's marvellous, wonderful.
SEMYON	Yes, you could look at it that way, if you pleased.
ARISTARKH	But shoot yourself as a responsible member of society. Please don't forget that you are not alone, look around you. *Semyon tries to look, still concealing gun* What do you see?
SEMYON	Nothing?
ARISTARKH	Take a look at our intelligentsia and what do you see?
SEMYON	Nothing.

ARISTARKH	And what do you hear? *Semyon shrugs* Nothing. And why? Because they are silent. And why are they silent? Because they are forced to be silent! But you can't silence a dead man, Comrade Podsekalnikov, if the dead man decides to talk. In these times the dead can say what the living only dare to think. I come to you as to a dead man, Comrade Podsekalnikov, I come to you in the name of the Russian intelligentsia.
SEMYON	Very pleased to meet you, please... have a seat.
ARISTARKH	You are right to take leave of this life, indeed this life is not worth living. But someone is to blame for this. I am not able to talk freely about this, but you can. You have nothing to lose now, nothing to fear, you are a free man now. And so, comrade, tell me honestly, who do you blame?
SEMYON	Who do I blame?
ARISTARKH	Don't be afraid.
SEMYON	Theodor Hugo Schultz.
ARISTARKH	That must be somebody from the Comintern — there's no doubt he's to blame. But, comrade, he's not the only one. The Government is full of men like him, it's useless to put all the blame on him alone.
SEMYON	Useless?
ARISTARKH	I'm afraid you still don't understand why you are shooting yourself. Allow me to explain.
SEMYON	Would you like some tea?
ARISTARKH	*Waving this aside* You want to die for the truth, Podsekalnikov, but the truth can't wait, you must do it quickly. Tear up this note immediately and write another one, write the truth. Defend us in it. Defend the intelligentsia and ask the government the ultimate question: why is such a sensitive, loyal and intelligent person — as Aristarkh Dominikovich Grand-Skubnik most certainly is — why is such a man not employed in the construction of a humane socialism?
SEMYON	Who?
ARISTARKH	Aristarkh Dominikovich Grand-Skubnik — with a hyphen.
SEMYON	Who's that?
ARISTARKH	Me... and when you have written such a note, comrade, then shoot yourself, and you die a hero. Your shot will be heard throughout Russia. And you POD-SE-KAL-NI-KOV, will awaken the sleeping conscience of the country.
SEMYON	I will?
ARISTARKH	Your name will become a household word. Your picture will appear on the front of every newspaper.
SEMYON	That would be better, my name's very difficult to spell.

ARISTARKH	The entire Russian intelligentsia will gather at your coffin, comrade. The elite of the nation will be your pall bearers, your hearse will be drowning in flowers and elegant horses with white pompoms will carry you to the cemetery.
SEMYON	What a life!
ARISTARKH	I would offer to commit suicide myself, comrade, but unfortunately I can't. I can't on principle. *Looks at his watch* So, it's all agreed. You are to compose a new suicide note, or better still, I will and you just sign it and shoot yourself.
SEMYON	No, I'll write it myself.
ARISTARKH	You are Pozharsky, you are Minin, comrade! In the name of the Russian intelligentsia permit me to embrace you. *Embraces him* I didn't cry when my own mother died, my poor mother, and now... and now... *Exits weeping*
SEMYON	*Tears in his eyes* Poor man... I will suffer, suffer for all of them, elegant horses with white pompoms... I will suffer for them who can't suffer for themselves! Where's the paper? *Searches* I'll expose our enemies, they haven't a chance. *Still searching* I will write the whole truth, just as it is, I've enough truth to fill the Volga! ...where, where, where? ...what a life! There's plenty of truth but no paper to write it on... *Goes to door, unlocks it* Masha? Masha? *Masha and Serafima enter. Semyon runs to put on vest, coat, and perhaps shoes*
MASHA	Where are you going?
SEMYON	To find paper! To find truth! Give me my hat and a ruble, Serafima — I must get some special paper, perhaps grey coloured with a gold border and my initials stamped across the top — hurry!
MASHA	Special paper?
SERAFIMA	Gold bordered?
SEMYON	And listen, Masha, you can't go around looking like that — I'm having visitors — the intelligentsia are coming, Masha, we have obligations.
MASHA	What should I do?
SEMYON	Put on some sort of brooch or at least wash your hair. Don't forget you're a Podsekalnikov — that means something. *Serafima hands him his hat and a ruble* Well, what are you standing there for, what are you two looking at? Hurry, hurry into the kitchen and get ready! *Exit Masha and Serafima. Semyon puts on hat, picks up piece of broken mirror, looks at himself* Actually Pozharsky does look a bit like me. So does Minin. But Minin less than Podharsky.
SERAFIMA	*Sticking her head in door* There's a woman here to see you,

	Semyon.
SEMYON	Send her in.
	Enter Cleopatra Maximovna
CLEOPATRA	Monsieur Podsekalnikov?
SEMYON	Oui, Madame, a votre service.
CLEOPATRA	*Holds out her hand* Cleoptra Maximovna, you can call me Cleo for short.
SEMYON	*Bowing* Mon Dieu.
CLEOPATRA	Now that we've made each other's acquaintance, I would like to ask a small favour of you.
SEMYON	With pleasure.
CLEOPATRA	Monsieur, since you are committing suicide anyway, why don't you be a sweetheart and do it for me.
SEMYON	How do you mean 'for you'?
CLEOPATRA	Don't be so selfish, monsieur, shoot yourself on my account.
SEMYON	Unfortnately I can't do that, I'm already committed.
CLEOPATRA	To whom? To Raisa Filipovna? Why? What's the matter with you? If you shoot yourself for that cow, then Oleg Leonidovich is going to dump me.
SEMYON	I'm sorry, I — won't you sit down?
CLEOPATRA	Better shoot yourself over me, then Oleg Leonidovich will dump her. That's because Oleg is an aesthete and Raisa Filipovna is only a bitch. I am telling you this because I am a romantic. She wants him to make love to her body and she herself wants to make love to his body, only his body, his body and his body alone. I on the other hand adore his soul and I want him to adore my soul, only my soul, my soul and my soul alone. Defend the soul, Monsieur Podsekalnikov, shoot yourself over me. Defend love! Then hundreds of young maidens will gather at your coffin, thousands of young men will carry you on their shoulders and beautiful women...
SEMYON	In white pompoms?
CLEOPATRA	Pardon?
SEMYON	Pardon, I'm getting carried away.
CLEOPATRA	What? Already? Control yourself, monsieur — no, no, please don't kiss me.
SEMYON	Believe me...
CLEOPATRA	I believe you — but clearly after this you will have to refuse Raisa Filipovna.
SEMYON	But I don't know any Raisa Filipovna.
CLEOPATRA	You don't? ...you will — she may be on her way here right now! She'll probably tell you that everyone is passionately in love with her stomach. She's always talking about it everywhere she goes. But it's not true, monsieur, she has an

	absolutely ordinary stomach. I assure you! And then again, a stomach is not a face! And a face — come closer... do you see something?
SEMYON	No.
CLEOPATRA	No?
SEMYON	My eyes, in the war I suffered...
CLEOPATRA	I have a very beautiful face.
SEMYON	I see.
CLEOPATRA	And if you can't see it here, then we can go over to my place and you'll see it there. I have a photograph of myself hanging over the bed. You'll be overwhelmed. And then you can write your note. Good, it's all agreed.
SEMYON	What note?
CLEOPATRA	I have real coffee as well.
SEMYON	What will I write?
CLEOPATRA	Everything that you feel — that I overwhelmed you with my charm and that you despaired of ever having those feelings returned and that is why you are shooting yourself.
SEMYON	Well...
CLEOPATRA	You're an aesthete, I can tell, an aristocrat of feeling, deep down you're a romantic like me, don't resist, let it flow out of you, naturally... *Enter Masha with a basin of water, soap and a sponge* ...you'll have to leave soon anyway, it looks like they're about to wash the floor.
MASHA	Not the floor, my hair.
CLEOPATRA	I wasn't talking to you, sweetie — who is this vulgar woman?
SEMYON	That's my... my... *Masha crosses to next room* ...my cook. *Enter Serafima, with broom and dustpan*
SERAFIMA	The samovar is on, perhaps the lady would like some tea?
SEMYON	No, no, no — listen, Serafima, why don't you tidy up this room a bit while I go and have real coffee with the lady. That's my... my... *Serafima crosses to next room* ...my cook's mother. I know they don't look like the usual hired help, but... people are never what they appear. *Enter Yegor, with letter*
YEGOR	You're right, Semyon...
SEMYON	Now who?
YEGOR	People are never what they appear.
SEMYON	Go away, Yegor! *to Cleoptara* He delivers the mail.
YEGOR	And I have become a writer to prove this point.
SEMYON	Well, let's go... *they exit*
YEGOR	Day after day of painstaking research and personal observation...

Finds himself alone, goes to keyhole, peeks through. Enter Serafima

SERAFIMA	What? What kind of pornography is this?
YEGOR	Hello, Serafima.
SERAFIMA	Masha's in there washing her hair and you're spying on her through a keyhole?
YEGOR	I'm looking at her from a Marxist point of view, Serafima, and there is no pornography in that point of view.
SERAFIMA	Are you suggesting that things look different from that point of view?
YEGOR	Not only different but completely reversed! I have tested out this theory on myself. For example, let's say you're walking down the street and coming towards you is a lady. Naturally the lady has certain proportions and curves... in a word beautiful, and you can't stand it! All you can do is shut your eyes and start panting. So you stop and think what happens if I look at her from a Marxist point of view? So you open your eyes and look. And what do you think happens, Serafima? This once gorgeous woman becomes so ugly I can't even tell you! In this world now there's nothing that I covet. I can look at everything from the Marxist point of view. Let me demonstrate — I'll look at you.
SERAFIMA	God forbid!
YEGOR	I'll do it anyway. *Closes his eyes*
SERAFIMA	Holy Mother have mercy!
	Enter Masha
MASHA	What's happening?
SERAFIMA	Yegor has reached the point.
MASHA	What point?
YEGOR	The Marxist one, Masha — hello!
MASHA	Are you here for business or pleasure?
YEGOR	I came to you, Masha, because of a comma.
SERAFIMA	A comma?
YEGOR	I have become a writer — I wrote a letter to the newspaper, but I don't know where to put the commas.
MASHA	Congratulations, when's the wedding?
YEGOR	What wedding?
SERAFIMA	Can Marxists marry?
MASHA	Once you've become a writer, it means you've fallen in love.
YEGOR	Me?
SERAFIMA	Of course, no wonder he's acting so peculiarly.
MASHA	It means you've been visited by the muse!
YEGOR	I admit it.
SERAFIMA	What's her name?
YEGOR	I was visited.

MASHA	And her name?
YEGOR	Alexander Petrovich Kalabushkin.
SERAFIMA	Congratulations, Yegor, you've gone nuts!
YEGOR	You're right, Serafima, I never planned to be a writer — but the moment I saw him I was lost. He inspires me so much, Masha, it's as if my hand is just welded to the pen and writes and writes and writes...
SERAFIMA	How does he inspire you?
YEGOR	Erotically.
MASHA	And what exactly did you write?
YEGOR	If you promise to tell me where the comma goes, I'll read it to you. It starts like this: *Reads* "To Comrade Editor of our newspaper from a postman of the Soviet Union. Scientists have proven that there are spots on the sun. And just such a spot in sexual matters is Alexander Petrovich Kalabushkin, the keeper of the 'Test Your Strength' machine and shooting gallery at the amusement park called 'The Red Beau-Monde'. Postmen don't need to test their strength, for we have already tested it during the civil war in which we fought for the freedom of the working class; but regarding the shooting gallery — it is closed all summer. The shooting gallery is closed but we postmen want to shoot. Moreover Alexander Petrovich Kalabushkin is never there arrogant bastard that he is but spends his evenings sitting in a nearby restaurant in the company of Margarita Ivanovna his eroticism fully revealed. We urge the editor to use his iron fist and take appropriate measures. Signed thirty-five thousand postmen."
MASHA	Did thirty-five thousand postmen really sign that?
YEGOR	No, I was the only one.
SERAFIMA	Then why...
YEGOR	That's my pen name.
MASHA	You've gone past the point, Yegor!
SERAFIMA	You ought to be ashamed, getting a good man into trouble over nothing.
	Enter Alexander
MASHA	Just in time! Alexander Petrovich, talk some sense into Yegor's head.
SERAFIMA	He has a problem.
ALEXANDER	No problem that can't be solved if we look at it logically, I'm sure.
YEGOR	The problem, comrade Kalabushkin, is where to put the comma... the sentence runs... '...is never there arrogant bastard that he is...' where does the comma go?
ALEXANDER	Before 'arrogant'.

YEGOR	Many thanks — I'm off to my editor. *Exit Yegor*
MASHA	You've just wiped out one person's illiteracy, but you will pay for it — do you know who the arrogant bastard is?
ALEXANDER	Who?
MASHA	You.
ALEXANDER	Me?
SERAFIMA	All down in black and white, about you and the shooting gallery and Margarita...
ALEXANDER	Run after him! Bring him back! No, I will! No you must! I've important business with Semyon. Hurry, run! My life's at stake! Tell him the shooting gallery will open right away! Run! Run! *Exit Masha and Serafima* The nerve... right to my face! ...now where is Semyon? *Alexander exits to kitchen. Enter Nikifor Pugachev*
PUGACHEV	No one home? *Enter Victor*
VICTOR	Are you Podsekalnikov?
PUGACHEV	Not me. *Enter Aristarkh Dominikovich*
VICTOR	You must be Podsekalnikov.
ARISTARKH	Certainly not!
PUGACHEV	*Giggling* Wrong again. *Re-enter Alexander*
ARISTARKH	Alexander Petrovich!
PUGACHEV & VICTOR	Comrade.
ARISTARKH	What are you doing here?
ALEXANDER	Gentlemen... *Enter Raisa Filipovna like a whirlwind*
RAISA	Kalabushkin, give me back my fifteen rubles at once!
ALEXANDER	Raisa, not in front of strangers.
RAISA	You cheated me! You filled my head with your Podsekalnikov! What did I give you fifteen rubles for? So that he could shoot himself over that other slut!
VICTOR	I gave you fifteen rubles!
ARISTARKH	What 'other slut'?
PUGACHEV	And I!
RAISA	What is this, a lottery? You promised him to me and now Cleopatra Maximovna has him!
VICTOR	He was promised to me!
ARISTARKH	*Making a note* Cleopatra Maximovna...
PUGACHEV	What did I pay for?
ALEXANDER	You paid for a chance, comrade, as indeed all of you did. What else do you pay for when you buy a lottery ticket? You

	pay for a chance!
ARISTARKH	I pay?
ALEXANDER	It's the same in this case of Podsekalnikov. You paid me to approach the proposed deceased, and you are not the only ones. Here, for example, are but a few of the notes that already exist — '...I am dying as a victim of nationalism' '...life is unbearable, in the event of my death no one is to blame except our beloved Soviet State...' and so on, and so forth. The various notes will be suggested to him, but which one he will choose I cannot say.
ARISTARKH	I can — he has already made his choice. He is shooting himself on behalf of the intelligentsia. I've just had a long chat with him in person.
ALEXANDER	That was most unethical of you, Aristarkh Dominikovich. You should have acted through me like all the other clients.
ARISTARKH	Your other clients will have to wait.
VICTOR	You can wait too!
ARISTARKH	The intelligentsia can't wait any longer.
PUGACHEV	And business in your opinion can?
VICTOR	And the arts?
ARISTARKH	Comrades, let me explain.
ALEXANDER	Darling Raisa, don't be angry with me.
ARISTARKH	In the present day and age the intelligentsia is the work horse of the proletariat.
VICTOR	In that case we artists are the scapegoats.
PUGACHEV	And we businessmen are the jackasses — what did I say? *Aristarkh and Victor laugh*
ALEXANDER	*To Raisa* I wouldn't disappoint you.
PUGACHEV	Why are you always harping on art? In this world business is also an art!
VICTOR	In this world art is also a business.
ARISTARKH	Comrades, we are all in business.
ALEXANDER	One hand helps the other, give up romance.
RAISA	Money?
ALEXANDER	Your dress shop outfits the funeral say?
RAISA	*Placing Alexander's hand on her breast* One hand helps the other.
ARISTARKH	Remember how it used to be, comrades? People used to have a cause and they wanted to die for that cause? Now people who want to die have no causes and those who have causes don't want to die. That's what we must fight against, each one of us.
ALEXANDER	Agreed!
ARISTARKH	Today more than ever we need ideological corpses! *Enter Semyon*

SEMYON	Are you all waiting for me?
ARISTARKH	These people have heard of your glorious decision, comrade, and so they came to show you their enthusiasm.
VICTOR	You are our last hope!
PUGACHEV	Our hero!
RAISA	A modern day saint!
SEMYON	Me?
RAISA	Don't be so modest.
ARISTARKH	When have you decided to shoot yourself?
SEMYON	I...
VICTOR	Let's say tomorrow.
ARISTARKH	Twelve noon — would that suit you?
SEMYON	Tomorrow?
PUGACHEV	*Starting to cry* Such courage!
ARISTARKH	I know you're anxious but, yes, postpone it till tomorrow.
PUGACHEV	*Crying* I can't stand it!
RAISA	We'll throw you a farewell party!
PUGACHEV	A banquet!
VICTOR	With liquor.
ALEXANDER	Margarita could arrange it.
RAISA	You'll be the guest of honour!
ARISTARKH	Would ten o'clock suit you?
SEMYON	That soon?
RAISA	You are modest.
ARISTARKH	For the banquet.
SEMYON	Oh the banquet, yes, that's fine.
ALEXANDER	So it's all agreed?
ARISTARKH	Tomorrow at noon you shoot yourself.
SEMYON	Tomorrow...
VICTOR	Your appointment's set.
SEMYON	My appointment? Who with?
ARISTARKH	With destiny — till tomorrow *Aside to Semyon* I'll be back.
VICTOR	I will write of you! *Aside* Later. *Exit*
ALEXANDER	The banquet's at ten...
RAISA	*Taking Alexander's hand* Tomorrow then! *They exit. Pause. Semyon and Pugachev alone.*
PUGACHEV	*Crying* Your courage... it's unbearable! *Exit*
SEMYON	Tomorrow... I must get my things together... my cigarette case... I'll send it to my brother... in Yelets, and my coat... to my brother... in Yelets... my striped pants, No! No... I'll wear them myself... for the banquet, striped pants are good for banquets. *Enter Serafima and Masha*
MASHA	Phew!
SERAFIMA	Hot!

MASHA	We just barely managed to catch Yegor...
SEMYON	Will you iron these pants for me, Serafima? And there's a little hole in them — I'm going to wear them tomorrow.
MASHA	Tomorrow?
SERAFIMA	Why wear out your good pants for nothing?
SEMYON	I have an appointment.
MASHA	Semyon, what are you saying?
SERAFIMA	Tomorrow?
MASHA	At last!
SERAFIMA	What time?
MASHA	What kind of job is it?
SEMYON	Twelve noon.
MASHA	We'll start to live again!
SERAFIMA	Is it temporary?
MASHA	*Embracing him* I can hardly believe it!
SEMYON	No, it's permanent.
MASHA	*Kisses his cheek* Tomorrow!
SERAFIMA	Where...?
MASHA	Mother, stop all those ridiculous questions and get the iron! *Embracing him* Oh thank God, Semyon.
SERAFIMA	Whatever it is, it's about time! *Exit*
SEMYON	Tomorrow I...
MASHA	We'll fix your pants right away and you'll have your eggnog with every meal... *Exit*
SEMYON	Just breakfast.
MASHA	*Offstage* Tomorrow!
SEMYON	Tomorrow... funny the things that bring us together... tomorrow I... if I do it at twelve on the dot, I wonder where I'll be at twelve thirty or even five to one? Not here... long journey or short? Who can answer? *A knock at the door* Again? ...Yes? *Enter Margarita with young boy carrying small suitcase and bundle*
MARGARITA	Semyon Semyonovich, would you mind if a friend sat with you for a while?
SEMYON	Who?
MARGARITA	This is Alexander Petrovich's nephew who's just arrived — from the provinces — but his uncle's door is locked — just let him sit here for a minute and I'll go and find Alexander Petrovich — he won't disturb you, he's a quiet boy, Semyon Semyonovich — from the provinces... *Exit*
SEMYON	Long journey? Short? Young man, do you think — or I should say what do you think — please don't interrupt, just listen — imagine that tomorrow at twelve noon you are

going to take a revolver in your hand — please don't interrupt me... Let us suppose that you then take the barrel and put it in your mouth — do you follow me? ...Let's say you put it in. You put it in. So you've put it in. And as soon as you've put it in, there's that moment. Let's look at that moment philosophically. What is a moment — tick tock? Yes, tick tock. And between the tick and the tock there's a barrier, yes a barrier, namely the barrel of the gun. Do you understand? Here's the barrel, here's the tick and there's the tock. On the tick side, young man, there's still everything, on the tock side there's already nothing. You squeeze the trigger and there's a loud bang bang the first bang is still tick but the second bang is already tock. Everything that concerns the tick-bang I understand but the tock-bang is a complete mystery to me. Do you understand? Tick and I'm still with myself and my wife and my mother-in-law and the sun and the fresh air and water — that I can understand. Tock and I'm without my wife — though I can understand being without a wife — and I'm without a mother-in-law, and that too I can understand completely, but to be without... say, without a pipe, black tobacco, borscht, blue fish, fresh cabbage, my fishing rod, my reversible coat, summer, sunflower seeds, a hard bed, birch trees, to be without myself? — that I cannot understand at all. How can I be without myself? Me, myself, Podsekal-nikov, a human being — let's look at this human being philosophically. Darwin proved to us, in the language of dry statistics, that man is a cage, please don't interrupt, I know what I'm saying, man is a cage. And the soul languishes in this cage. That I can understand. You shoot yourself, and that shot breaks the cage and the soul flies out, and it flies and flies and naturally as it's flying it's crying: 'Hosanna! Hosanna!' and naturally God calls it over and asks: To whom do you belong? To Podsekalnikov. Did you suffer? Yes... in that case go and have a good time, and the soul begins to dance and sing, doesn't it? All that I understand. How could I not understand it! ...what then? What do you think? Is there life after death? I'm asking you a question. *Shaking him* Is there or isn't there! Yes or no! Answer me!
Enter Margarita

MARGARITA   Thank you very much Semyon Semyonovich — I found a spare key to the room. Isn't he good? Poor boy! Well-behaved? He's a deaf mute — what can you do? Thank you again... *They exit*

SEMYON   Tomorrow...

END OF ACT II

the SUICIDE

ACT III

ACT III	*A restaurant under an open sky in the amusement park. At tables: Alexander Petrovich, Grand-Skubnik, Pugachev, Victor, Margarita, Cleopatra, Raisa, guests — they are toasting Semyon. Semyon is entangled in paper streamers and covered in confetti. A waiter hands a glass of wine to Semyon on the back of a guitar. Everyone toasts. Semyon drains his glass, then throws it over his shoulder. The guests applaud.*

PUGACHEV	Bravo!
RAISA	That's the way.
CLEOPATRA	That's why we love you, Semyon Semyonovich.
MARGARITA	Don't worry about the cost, Semyon. Kostya, Kostya darling. *Waiter runs to table*
PUGACHEV	*To Semyon* Have one on me.
MARGARITA	*To Waiter* Put down ninety kopeks for the glass to Alexander Petrovich — drink everyone! What's the matter, Semyon?
SEMYON	What time is it?
MARGARITA	Twelve's a long way away.
SEMYON	A long way?
MARGARITA	Away — don't think about it, drink.
VICTOR	*To Cleopatra* Pushkin once went to the bathhouse...
CLEOPATRA	Don't talk to me of Pushkin, you know I can't stand obscene stories.
SEMYON	Waiter?
WAITER	At your service?
SEMYON	What time is it?
WAITER	Close to twelve.
SEMYON	Close?
WAITER	Close.
	Semyon takes drink from tray
PUGACHEV	Waiter!
VICTOR	*To Raisa* Pushkin once went to the bathhouse...
RAISA	*Begins to laugh* Oh Pushkin! Oh, I can't! ...Wait, let me visualize every detail... *Closes her eyes* bathhouse, rough wood, windy chinks, peepholes — I see it! So?
VICTOR	So Pushkin went to the bathhouse...
ARISTARKH	Honoured guests, we are gathered here to say farewell to a dear friend, Semyon Semyonovich, who is leaving us — disconsolate — for a better world.

VICTOR	From whose bourn no traveller returns.
ARISTARKH	Please don't interrupt me.
VOICES	Quiet, quiet... ssshhhh.... *A dead silence*
VICTOR	Then Pushkin takes off his pants...
	Raisa screeches with laughter
VOICES	Quiet, quiet...!
RAISA	I see it.
ARISTARKH	Friends, have I known courage? Have I known truth? Have I known beauty before this? The path you have chosen, Semyon Semyonovich... *Choked with tears* What can I say? ...Others will follow.
RAISA	*Laughing* I see it. Red breeches and spindly shanks.
ARISTARKH	Many brave and youthful heads will turn to your example — then fathers will cry, then mothers will collapse before the familiar corpse, and our homeland will shudder — and the gates of the Kremlin will be flung open and our government will come out to us 'in corpore' and offer its hand to the merchant, and the merchant will offer his hand to the worker, and the worker will offer his hand to the farmer, and the farmer will offer his hand to the intelligentsia, and the intelligentsia will — no, that's where it will stop.
VICTOR	So Pushkin gave it to her 'in corpore'.
ARISTARKH	I drink to your honour, Semyon Semyonovich! Hip... Hip...
ALL	Hooray!
SEMYON	Dearly beloved...
VOICES	Shhhh...
ALEXANDER	*Pounding table* Attention! Attention! *A dead silence* Now you can speak, Semyon Semyonovich.
SEMYON	What time is it?
MARGARITA	Don't think about it, drink.
CLEOPATRA	Let's have a happy song! *Music begins*
PUGACHEV	Another cheer! Hip... Hip...
ALL	Hooray!
ARISTARKH	I didn't cry when my own mother died, dear comrades, and now... and now...
PUGACHEV	Aristarkh Dominikovich, I am a simple butcher, but I would like to say that you expresed yourself beautifully — it would be a wonderful thing if the government stretched out their hands to butchers.
VICTOR	It would be even better if they were stretched out in their coffins.
ALEXANDER	Waiter! Champagne for my friend.
RAISA	I can visualize every detail — the dictatorship, the republic, the revolution — but who really needs it?

VICTOR	Who? How can you ask such a question? I can't imagine myself without a Soviet republic.
ALEXANDER	I agree with everything. Champagne!
CLEOPATRA	*To Victor* Then you are satisfied?
VICTOR	Alas, no.
CLEOPATRA	*To Raisa* I didn't think so.
SEMYON	What time is it?
VICTOR	*To Raisa* I want a small something to be added to our Soviet republic.
RAISA	*Laughing* Is it obscene?
VICTOR	I want to ride in my sledge over the steppe to the tinkle of silver bells in the morning light, wearing my beaver hat cocked back, surrounded by gypsies, at knee my favourite dog.
CLEOPATRA	I loathe Gogol.
VOICES	Shhhh! Shhhh!
VICTOR	I want a guitar string to break!
CLEOPATRA	Poor Chekhov.
MARGARITA	Anton Pavlovich?
VOICES	Sshhhh! Shhhh!
VICTOR	I want the coachman to weep into his homespun mittens, I want to toss my hat into the air, to fall into a snowdrift, to pray, to curse, to repent, then have a good drink, then shout till my voice is one with the universe and I fly! But I want to do it our way, the Russian way, so that the soul is torn out and tossed to the devil, he can keep it! All I want is the earth to spin like a child's top under the runners of my sledge, I want my magnificent horses to lift from the earth and spread like birds over the fields, and the troika no longer a troika but Russia, all of Russia racing onward inspired by God. Oh, Russia, where are you racing? Where? *Enter Yegor*
YEGOR	Straight to the police.
ALEXANDER	To the police?
RAISA	What for?
YEGOR	Because it's against the law to drive that fast, you're only allowed to do fifty miles an hour.
VICTOR	Is that your idea of a metaphor?
YEGOR	Allow me to give you some advice. The only metaphor that is permitted is the one that conforms to the law. In fact, socialism is not interested in metaphors; all I'm interested in is whether the shooting gallery is open or not.
ALEXANDER	It was, Yegor. We waited for you.
MARGARITA	Have a drink, Yegor.
YEGOR	I don't drink.

ALEXANDER	Why not?
YEGOR	It's a bad habit.
ALEXANDER	What's so bad about it? Try it.
YEGOR	No, I'm afraid.
CLEOPATRA	Afraid?
YEGOR	What if you get used to it and then socialism comes along and under socialism there's no more wine — try and get around that one.
CLEOPATRA	Just one glass, for the women.
YEGOR	Furthermore, under socialism there won't be any more women.
VICTOR	Nonsense, men can't live without women.
YEGOR	Under socialism there won't be any more men.
VICTOR	No more men? What will there be?
YEGOR	Masses, masses, and more masses — an enormous mass of masses.
ALEXANDER	Then have a drink for the masses.
YEGOR	All right then, for the masses.
VICTOR	Fill his glass.
RAISA	More music!
ALEXANDER	How is it?
YEGOR	I like it when people fuss over me — nowadays everybody busies themselves with crap.
VICTOR	Namely who?
YEGOR	Namely you — tell me, writer, what do you write about?
VICTOR	About everything.
YEGOR	Tolstoy also wrote about everything — that doesn't impress me. I'm a postman and I want to read about postmen. Understand?
SEMYON	Tell me, Yegor, in your opinion is there life after death?
YEGOR	There might be, but under socialism there won't be, I can guarantee that.
MARGARITA	Why are you standing, Semyon? Come over here, sit next to me.
CLEOPATRA	*To Yegor* I am Cleopatra Maximovna.
YEGOR	I know.
RAISA	Oleg Leonidovich told me straight out, 'I can't get your beautiful stomach out of my head'.
ALEXANDER	To the health of the masses, Yegor.
YEGOR	I can't refuse.
MARGARITA	Don't eat so much, better to drink, Semyon Semyonovich.
CLEOPATRA	*To Yegor* You haven't seen anything of life, I can tell. There is another life out there, with linens, furniture, furs, cosmetics. Admit it, are you never drawn away from here to, let's say, Paris?

YEGOR	I admit it, I'm drawn — I even started saving money.
CLEOPATRA	For a trip?
YEGOR	For a tower.
CLEOPATRA	Ah, the Eiffel Tower.
YEGOR	And as soon as I get to Paris I climb to the top of this tower and look down on Paris, from a Marxist point of view.
CLEOPATRA	And then what?
YEGOR	I won't want to live in Paris any more.
CLEOPATRA	Why not?
YEGOR	You cannot understand me because you are a woman from the upper class.
ARISTARKH	What do you mean by that? Who in your opinion made the revolution?
YEGOR	I did. I mean, we did.
ARISTARKH	That's a narrow view, Yegor — permit me to give you my opinion by means of an allegory.
YEGOR	What kind of an allegory?
ARISTARKH	An allegory from the animal kingdom.
VOICES	Quiet! Quiet! Please...
MARGARITA	Don't listen, drink, Semyon.
ARISTARKH	Some duck eggs were placed under a warm-hearted hen. And she sat on them for many years and warmed them with her body till finally one day the ducklings pecked their way out of the eggs and jubilantly crawled out from under the hen, grabbed her by the scruff of the neck and dragged her to the river. 'I am your mother!' cried the hen. 'What are you doing!' 'Swim!' roared the ducks. Do you understand the allegory?
VOICES	Not really... No... Not entirely.
ARISTARKH	The long-suffering hen is our intelligentsia.
YEGOR	Agreed.
ARISTARKH	And the eggs? The proletariat. Many we sat on the proletariat...
YEGOR	Many years...
ARISTARKH	And the proletariat pecked their way out of the eggs, grabbed the intelligentsia and dragged her to the river.
CLEOPATRA	Do you swim, Yegor?
ARISTARKH	I am your mother! We cried.
VICTOR	Unlikely.
YEGOR	Then swim, roar the ducks, yes, yes.
ARISTARKH	'I can't swim!' the intelligentsia said.
VICTOR	Then fly!
ARISTARKH	Ah, but a hen is not a bird.
YEGOR	Then what?
ARISTARKH	Then sit, and they actually sat the hend down. My brother-

	in-law, for example, has been sitting for five years in prison. Do you understand the allegory now?
RAISA	He was probably arrested for embezzling government funds.
ARISTARKH	Money is a minor detail. Answer me, he among you who can, why did we nurture them? With all our talents, with our clear and piercing minds, why?
ALEXANDER	Wherever the head is, the ass won't be far behind.
MARGARITA	What?
ARISTARKH	What would you have made of all those eggs, Semyon Semyonovich?
SEMYON	Eggnog.
ARISTARKH	Pearls of wisdom!
VICTOR	You mean allegorically?
SEMYON	Tell me, comrades, is there life after death?
VICTOR	According to science there isn't.
RAISA	According to socialism?
YEGOR	There isn't.
SEMYON	According to the truth?
ALEXANDER	Nobody knows.
SEMYON	Then there's no point in asking.
PUGACHEV	In half an hour you'll know.
SEMYON	In half an hour?
ALEXANDER	Don't think about it...
MARGARITA	Drink, Semyon.
SEMYON	Half an hour? Already? ...Sing me off, dear comrades. Give me music. Sing. Sing you bastards.
VOICES	Sing! Sing! Hooray!
SEMYON	Life begins half an hour before death!
YEGOR	To the health of the masses!
SEMYON	Masses? Listen to me! Listen to Podsekalnikov!
RAISA	We're listening!
PUGACHEV	Bravo!
CLEOPATRA	Our leader!
VICTOR	Speak!
SEMYON	I am dying now.
ARISTARKH	And who is to blame?
SEMYON	The leaders are to blame!
ARISTARKH	And why?
YEGOR	Is this another allegory?
SEMYON	Walk up to any leader and ask him, 'What have you done for Podsekalnikov?' And he won't answer, comrades, because he doesn't even know that a Podsekalnikov exists.
ARISTARKH	A good point.
SEMYON	He exists, dear comrades, and I am he. In half an hour I will

	take my life and toss it away. I will die and then no one, no one will stop me from talking, from the Caucasus to the Neva I will tell everyone that I am dying for... for...
ARISTARKH	For?
VOICES	Yes? Our hero, yes?
SEMYON	How can I tell them what I'm dying for, comrades, if I haven't even read my own suicide note?
ARISTARKH	We'll arrange everything, comrade.
ALEXANDER	An extra table and chair, Margarita!
MARGARITA	Kostya! A table!
ARISTARKH	Give him room, comrades.
	Bodies press forward with notes in hand. The waiters bring table and chair. On table there is paper, a vase with flowers, champagne, a work lamp with green shade.
ALEXANDER	Stand back, this is the most important moment of his life!
ARISTARKH	Read this, Podsekalnikov.
SEMYON	What's this?
ARISTARKH	It's all written.
ALEXANDER	Everything is under control, comrades.
SEMYON	'Why I cannot go on living'. That's it, thank you, how can I ever repay you!
ARISTARKH	Sit down and copy it.
ALEXANDER	We won't disturb you, Semyon Semyonovich. Quiet, everyone!
VOICES	Quiet! Quiet!
ALEXANDER	Waiter! Ask the maestro for a soft waltz. *Music*
SEMYON	*Copying* 'Why I cannot go on living, exclamation mark. People and members of the party, look into the eyes of history' — that's very good — 'look into the eyes of history' — excellent! sheer beauty!
VICTOR	It's frightening how much we writers love beauty — but when the censor lifts his red pen we go pale.
RAISA	You're going to throw up, I told you so.
SEMYON	*Reads* 'Because we were all touched by the cleansing whirlwind of the revolution.' Exclamation mark. Underlined in red. *Copies*
CLEOPATRA	I am sick of this dull life. I want dissonance, Yegor Timofeevich.
RAISA	*To Cleopatra* Were you talking to me before?
CLEOPATRA	No.
RAISA	You bore me.
SEMYON	*Reads* 'Remember that the intelligentsia is the salt of the earth and if they cease to exist you will have nothing with which to salt your pot in which you are stewing.' Let's see... Remember... *Copies*

VICTOR	We could work together, Aristarkh Dominokovich.
ARISTARKH	We? What do you mean?
VICTOR	You have your corpse, but who will know? I am a writer...
ARISTARKH	I see.
ALEXANDER	And I distribute the word to the masses.
ARISTARKH	For a fee?
SEMYON	Exclamation mark. That is what I am dying for, comrades. Signed. *Pugachev begins to weep*
MARGARITA	Why are you crying?
PUGACHEV	I'm unhappy.
MARGARITA	Drink.
SEMYON	Comrades!
VOICES	He's finished... Is he finished? ...Shhhh!
SEMYON	Do you know what I can do? *Pugachev sobs loudly* Thanks to you I can stop being afraid. At this moment I am not afraid of anyone, I can do whatever I like — what does it matter? In half an hour...
ALEXANDER	Ten minutes...
SEMYON	Oh God, I can do anything! For the first time in my life I'm not unhappy, I'm not afraid — there are two hundred million people in the Soviet Union, comrades, and each one is afraid of someone — two hundred million fears, but I'm not afraid of anyone! Hold me back, comrades, or I'll start dancing. Today I have power over everyone. I am a dictator. I am a czar. I can do anything, anything.
ARISTARKH	*To Alexander* How much longer?
ALEXANDER	Five minutes.
SEMYON	What should I do? Comrades, what can I do for all of you? How can I free you?
CLEOPATRA	For me? *Embracing Yegor*
RAISA	For me? *Embracing Victor*
SEMYON	I've got it! How glorious. I'll call the Kremlin!
RAISA	What?!
SEMYON	Straight to the red heart of the Soviet Union.
ARISTARKH	For God's sake!
CLEOPATRA	Don't do it.
SEMYON	And curse the hell out of the sons of bitches there. *Goes to booth*
ALEXANDER	Stop him.
MARGARITA	Hide!
VICTOR	We're all dead!
SEMYON	Shut up! Everyone must be silent when a Colossus speaks with a Colossus. Get me the Kremlin, don't be afraid, operator — who? The Kremlin? Oh, Podsekalnikov — no, I'm a private person — Podsekalnikov!

44

VICTOR	*To Semyon* For art's sake...
SEMYON	Well get someone on the line, anyone, the yo-yo at the top — I don't care!
CLEOPATRA	*To Semyon* For beauty's sake...
SEMYON	No one there? Well then give him this message...
ALEXANDER	*To Semyon* For everyone's sake!
SEMYON	Tell him I read Marx and I didn't like him. Don't interrupt me!
YEGOR	Tell them their socialism stinks.
SEMYON	Then tell him to go take a running jump. Do you hear? Oh my God!
	Dumbfounded, Semyon drops the receiver
ARISTARKH	What happened?
SEMYON	They hung up.
VICTOR	What?
YEGOR	Who did they hang?
SEMYON	The receiver. Comrades, they're afraid of me. I can hardly believe it. The Kremlin is afraid of me; what do I represent? It's almost terrifying to analyse it. Think about it comrades — from childhood on I always wanted to be a genius, but my parents were against it. What did I live for? To end up a statistic? How many years has life been mocking me? And look at me now. How many years has life slapped me in the face? But no more! Today, this hour, this minute, this second, this split second, this instant... Life! I demand satisfaction!
	The clock strikes twelve. Dead silence.
MARGARITA	Get ready, Semyon Semyonovich.
SEMYON	Already? Isn't your watch fast?
ALEXANDER	We set ours by the post office.
ARISTARKH	Everyone sit down, according to custom.
SEMYON	What custom? *All sit. Pause.* I was never much for customs... Well, farewell, comrades.
	Semyon goes to exit. Returns. Takes bottle
	Excuse me... courage...
	Goes to exit. Enter Waiter with tray of drinks
WAITER	Come again, Semyon Semyonovich.
SEMYON	No — it's your turn to come to me. *Exit*
	All are still. Pugachev is sniffling

END OF ACT III

the SUICIDE

ACT IV

ACT IV   *Podsekalnikov's apartment.*
          Serafima is beating eggnog in a glass, while singing a
          lullaby. Masha, offstage, joins in singing.

SERAFIMA   'Sleep my young...'
MASHA   Mother?
SERAFIMA   Yes?
          Enter Masha with kerosene lamp and curling irons in hand
MASHA   Do you think Semyon would like my hair better with tight
          curls or soft waves?
SERAFIMA   Who can tell?
MASHA   Well, which would you guess?
SERAFIMA   Do the front in soft waves and the back in curls, that way
          you can't go wrong. *Sings* 'Sleep my young...'
MASHA   You're a great help.
SERAFIMA   *Smiling* I am. *Hums*
MASHA   How long will you take? He'll be back any minute.
SERAFIMA   I put in two yolks for one glass of eggnog.
MASHA   *Smiling* You didn't!
          She tastes some on end of finger
          Mmm! Isn't it a sin the way he loves eggnog!
SERAFIMA   Let him enjoy himself today. *Sings*
MASHA   I'm so happy today!
SERAFIMA   *Sings* 'Friends in a raging tempest'.
MASHA   ˈ I hope the job works out.
SERAFIMA   Why wouldn't it?
MASHA   They can say there's no work and that's that.
SERAFIMA   How can there be no work in Russia? There's enough work
          here for all of humanity! You just have to know how to go
          about getting it.
MASHA   Then why isn't everyone working?
SERAFIMA   Because of 'pull'.
MASHA   'Pull'?
SERAFIMA   Now there's a sin for you! Plenty of work but not enough
          'pull' for each job.
MASHA   I don't understand.
SERAFIMA   Let's say there's a job but there's no one to pull strings for
          that job, then that position never gets filled! But since our
          Semyon already has pull, then there'll be no problem
          finding a job.
MASHA   We'll start living again!
SERAFIMA   Of course we'll start living again. *Sings*

MASHA	Thank you, Mother... *Seeing letter on table* What's this?
SERAFIMA	An old letter — throw it out.
MASHA	No, it's sealed... addressed to you.
SERAFIMA	Then read it to me, Mashenka.
MASHA	*Reads* 'My dearest Serafima Ilynichna, by the time you read this letter, I will no longer be among the living. Break the news gently to Masha.'
SERAFIMA	God in heaven!
MASHA	Wait! *Reads* 'My reversible coat and cigarette case are to be sent to my brother in Yelets. Semyon.' What's this?
SERAFIMA	Suicide?
MASHA	What's happening?
SERAFIMA	Again?
MASHA	Oh my God! *Falls on bed weeping* Oh my God!
SERAFIMA	Masha dear, don't cry, for God's sake!
	Door flies open and in walk Alexander, Aristarkh Dominikovich, Margarita, Raisa, and Seamstress
ALEXANDER	Weep, weep, widow Podsekalnikov! I understand, my dear — do I understand, Margarita? — the dirt still on my shoes from my wife's grave, I understand, widow, do I understand?
MARGARITA	*To Alexander* You've made your point.
ARISTARKH	Allow me... widow Podsekalnikov, I ask you a small favour in the name of the Russian intelligentsia. Your husband is dead, but his body is shining with life. Semyon Semyonovich is alive among us as a social symbol. Let us sustain that life amongst us! I've finished.
ALEXANDER	Raisa Filipovna, please attend to your duties.
RAISA	Would you prefer an ordinary straw hat or a lace one?
MASHA	*Crying* Leave me alone!
RAISA	Or perhaps one in felt?
MASHA	*Crying* I'm all alone!
RAISA	I have here an absolutely elegant hat — a touch more dear than the others...
MARGARITA	But just perfect for a funeral.
MASHA	Leave me alone!
MARGARITA	There's no point in carrying on like that, Masha.
SERAFIMA	Masha, Masha, ssshhh, there, there!
MARGARITA	The funeral's going to be quite chic, why should you look worse than anyone else?
SERAFIMA	Chic? And where are we going to get the money to bury him?
ALEXANDER	Everything's taken care of, Serafima...
RAISA	We'll begin the fitting!
MASHA	Don't touch me!

ALEXANDER	Everything from the burial to the mourning dress.
MASHA	Friends!
ARISTARKH	*Taking Masha in hand* No need for tears, widow Podsekalnikov, your husband died a hero! Why are you crying?
MASHA	How can I go on living?
ARISTARKH	I'll tell you, Masha, ssshhh, sshhh, quiet... live like your husband died, for he died in a manner worthy of imitation.
RAISA	*Taking measurements* Front length: forty-one.
ARISTARKH	Alone, he took his gun in his hand, and set out on the path of our Russian intelligentsia.
RAISA	Back length: ninety-four.
ARISTARKH	For he fell on the road and there he lies.
SERAFIMA	Where?
ARISTARKH	On the path of history.
SERAFIMA	Is that far from here?
ALEXANDER	Quite far.
ARISTARKH	There he lies, a terrifying stumbling block.
RAISA	Would you care for any trim?
ARISTARKH	And he who walks along this path will stumble upon our Podeskalnikov!
RAISA	And here's the hat.
SERAFIMA	Poor Semyon!
RAISA	Slightly on the whimsical side. We can make it out of crepe...
SERAFIMA	*To Raisa* No, felt.
RAISA	Felt, sprinkled with tiny bluebells.
ARISTARKH	And when he stumbles, widow, he will naturally look down at his feet and he will see us.
RAISA	Just try this one on.
ARISTARKH	And we will tell him — you who are treading the path of history, you — the nation builder — take a closer look at the body of Podsekalnikov!
SERAFIMA	*To Masha* Down! Down!
MARGARITA	Now to the side!
RAISA	Exquisite!
ARISTARKH	Then he will look and ask — what is the meaning of this body? And we will pause a moment, and then say to him...
RAISA	Do you want the skirt pleated?
ARISTARKH	This is our critique of your work.
RAISA	Or full?
ARISTARKH	Yes, widow, stand with your shoulders back! Head up! Your husband died a hero!
MASHA	Can I have both?
ALEXANDER	Honour and glory to the wife of our dearly departed!

SERAFIMA	Is Semyon a mess?
ARISTARKH	I couldn't look.
ALEXANDER	From compassion, none of us could.
SERAFIMA	Where's the body now?
RAISA	Everything'll be ready at three.
MARGARITA	*To Serafima* The butcher has him.
ALEXANDER	Everything, wreaths, coffin, clergy, everything.
ARISTARKH	We will leave you now, but we will return; we will not abandon you in your hour of need. Be of good cheer. *Enter Pugachev, muttering and crying, dragging the lifeless body of Semyon* I didn't cry when my poor mother died... *Sees the body, turns away* My own mother! *Exits*
ALEXANDER	*To Serafima* Wash the body down, will you? It probably needs it. *Raisa, Margarita, Alexander and Seamstress turn away in horror and exit. Masha shrieks the moment she sees the body, falls to her knees and cradles Semyon, somewhat reminiscent of the Pieta. Serafima falls to her knees and prays*
MASHA	Semyon!!
SERAFIMA	Merciful God!
PUGACHEV	*Crying* I didn't want to...
MASHA	I don't care if I live or die!
PUGACHEV	I didn't want him to die!
MASHA	What good is this damned life!
SERAFIMA	Holy Mother...
MASHA	What good is this damned hat!
PUGACHEV	I couldn't help it.
MASHA	When I had Semyon I had no hat!
PUGACHEV	*Exiting* Forgive me. Forgive. *Exits*
MASHA	Now I've a hat and no Semyon!
SERAFIMA	We didn't take care of him!
MASHA	I have been punished!
SERAFIMA	And, God help us, he died!
SEMYON	Died? Who died? Died? Hold me up!
MASHA & SERAFIMA	Help!
SEMYON	I'm flying! I'm flying! Hosanna!
MASHA	Semyon! *Grabs him. Tussle begins*
SEMYON	Hosanna!
SERAFIMA	Semyon! *Grabs him*
SEMYON	Get behind me Satan!
MASHA	Semyon!

Serafima has Semyon's arms pinned from behind; he flaps his legs

SEMYON	I'm flying! Flying!
MASHA	*Holding his legs still* Semyon!
SEMYON	Who is it?
MASHA	Me!
SEMYON	Mother of God!
MASHA	Semyon, as God is with you!
SEMYON	God? With me? Excuse me, I didn't recognize you.
MASHA	He's gone mad!
SEMYON	May I introduce myself, I am the soul of Podsekalnikov.
SERAFIMA	Semyon, what happened?!
SEMYON	Father? I suffered, don't think that I'm lying, Father.
SERAFIMA	I'm not your father, I'm your mother-in-law.
SEMYON	Oh grief! You too. When did you die?
SERAFIMA	Smell his breath. *Masha does so*
SEMYON	Serafima, what happens now?
MASHA	He's drunk!
SERAFIMA	*Releasing him* Congratulations!
MASHA	*Rising* This is too much.
SEMYON	Where does one join the heavenly hosts?
MASHA	You bastard. You leave a note saying you're committing suicide...
SERAFIMA	And then you have the nerve to go out and get drunk!
SEMYON	Wait a minute!
SERAFIMA	No, you wait a minute.
SEMYON	You son of a bitch, the agony you caused me.
SEMYON	Am I alive?
MASHA	You want to lead me to an early grave?
SEMYON	Sounds like it.
SERAFIMA	And me with anemia...
SEMYON	I am.
MASHA	Why don't you say something?
SEMYON	What time is it?
MASHA	What time? I'll give you a time...!
SERAFIMA	*Restraining Masha* About two.
SEMYON	Oh God. Two!
MASHA	And you're drunk.
SEMYON	*To heavens* Thank you!
SERAFIMA	In the middle of the afternoon.
SEMYON	Just to give me courage, believe me, I drank and drank, it's true, but only for courage. At noon I went behind a tree, gun in my hand, and I drank.
MASHA	*Crying* Was your life that bad?
SEMYON	And still I couldn't do it. I raised the gun, or I raised the

53

	bottle? But suddenly the gun went off, both fell to the ground, that I remember, or I fell to the ground? Something fell to the ground. Why can't I remember?
MASHA	I can't believe your life with me was that miserable.
SEMYON	*To himself* Where are the others?
SERAFIMA	*To Semyon* But life with you and your friends is another story!
SEMYON	Has anyone come over yet?
SERAFIMA	Crowds of them!
SEMYON	What did they do?
SERAFIMA	They spoke, gave their condolences.
MASHA	We'll pay for everything, they said, your husband died a hero! — if only they knew.
SEMYON	Good God!
SERAFIMA	They're sewing her mourning dress this very moment.
MASHA	Oh no! They'll want their money back.
SEMYON	What money?
SERAFIMA	Our money!
SEMYON	I might as well be dead.
MASHA	We'll have to tell them the truth. Let's go, Mother, hurry!
SEMYON	Wait! All is not lost! I can still shoot myself.
SERAFIMA	He's starting again.
MASHA	Pay no attention. *To Semyon* Why don't you do something useful for a change — let's hurry, Mother.
SEMYON	I will, you'll see.
MASHA	Put the kettle on for tea. *Exit Masha and Serafima*
SEMYON	They don't believe me, after all I've been through, they still don't believe me. All right! *Takes out gun* Do it quickly, don't think, right in the heart, done. *Presses gun to chest* Maybe not, maybe in the mouth, quicker, you'll see, Masha! *Puts gun in mouth* I'll count to three... one, two... *Re-enter Masha and Serafima. Semyon hides gun behind back*
MASHA	What do I say? What do I say?
SERAFIMA	*To Semyon* They're down the street, wreaths, coffin, a truck!
SEMYON	I'll shoot myself.
MASHA	Oh damn — the truth can't be that difficult. *Leaving*
SERAFIMA	*Following* They're friends! *Exit Masha and Serafima*
SEMYON	The end... *Puts gun in mouth, tries to count, takes gun out* maybe not. If I'm going to count I better aim for the heart *To his chest* one, two, I'll count to twenty, one, two, three, what a coward! Decisively to ten, one, two, three... four... faster! Ten could take forever! To five, one... two... three... four... maybe it's better not to count at all. Then through the

mouth... *Into mouth ... takes it out* pity to spoil the head, better the heart, and a quick count, one, two — to five — three, four — to ten — six, seven, eight, my heart's stopped! No it hasn't — aim in the right place, where is it? Aim where it's beating, here and here, it's beating here, here, God it's beating! I'm going to explode! Wait! — if I die of a heart attack, I won't be able to commit suicide, I have to live! Ridiculous — one, two, three, four, five, I won't make it, six, seven, I'm suffocating, eight, nine, shoot! Ten! Shoot you bastard! Shoot anywhere!

Revolver jumps out of his hand and falls

MASHA   *Offstage* Hurry! Hurry!

SEMYON   Too late, I'm dying!

                Semyon faints. Enter Masha and Serafima

MASHA   If it's so easy...

SERAFIMA   Who said easy?

MASHA   Why don't you tell them!?

SERAFIMA   Why doesn't Semyon!?

MASHA   *Seeing him* Semyon?

SERAFIMA   Oh my God! Semyon?

                Masha and Serafima approach body cautiously. Enter Victor, with many wreaths

MASHA   Semyon?

VICTOR   Eloquent remembrances from his friends...

                Starts to put wreaths down carefully

MASHA   Semyon, wake up!

SERAFIMA   Son of a bitch! Enough is enough!

                Enter Alexander with wreaths. Victor standing transfixed

MASHA   You bastard!

SERAFIMA   Wake up!

ALEXANDER   It's their way, I understand — they must.

                Alexander throws wreaths down, pulls Victor out of room Have you never seen death before? *They exit*

SEMYON   *Coming to* Another miracle!

MASHA   Oh thank God! — you bastard...

SERAFIMA   *Seeing wreaths* What's this?

MASHA   This must stop, stop, stop! — dammit, I'll tell them — I'll tell Alexander Petrovich first, he'll help me! *Going*

SERAFIMA   *Reading ribbon* 'To the unforgettable Semyon, fighter and son-in-law.'

MASHA   Come with me, Mother! *Exits*

SERAFIMA   'From your mother-in-law who is stricken with grief'. *Going* Very true. My lot. Always. *Exits*

SEMYON   *Reading ribbon* 'Don't say that he is dead. He lives. Yours, Raisa'. Oh my God, she guessed it. Damn her. Where's my

gun? Hurry! *Picks up gun, points at chest* you say he lives...
all right... *Puts gun in mouth* you'll see how he lives... you'll
see... *Points gun at temple* Rest in peace, fighter and... no,
this can't be! I won't be rushed. Funeral or no funeral, I'll sit
down with a newspaper and rest... then I'll have the
strength to start over... *He sits down with paper* My mother
always said I'd be late for my own funeral... *He reads* 'The
state of international affairs' — the state of international
crap! ...what's that compared with the state of affairs of a
single human being.

Turns page and reads

'On the corner of Semyonovsky and Barabanny an
unknown citizen was run over by a street car' ...that's what I
call luck! He was out walking, not thinking about it at all,
and suddenly — dead. I think too much, far too much — I
must relax, distract myself, get into a good mood, and then
— bang, like a street car, the end. Yes, yes, yes... pretend
everything is wonderful, clear blue sky, sun, not thinking of
anything in particular, the birds are singing, you are
singing, humming a tune...

Hums, slowly brings gun toward temple

not a care in the world...

*Hand stops, lowers; Semyon quickly goes to mirror, drapes
black cloth over it, returns*

Everything calm, and in its proper place... on a park bench,
reading the paper... *Hand starts to rise* voices on the busy
street...

Sound of voices, muffled, offstage, growing louder

street cars and traffic, bicycle bells, ting ting — ting ting...
He hums, hand stops a funeral passes...

*Suddenly the door flies open, coffin flies in, followed by
Victor and Pugachev; all land with a crash. Semyon, caught,
simply lowers his head, hides gun under newspaper on his
lap*

VICTOR & PUGACHEV	Heave! Heave!
PUGACHEV	Made it!
VICTOR	Over here. *Places coffin on table*
PUGACHEV	*Seeing Semyon* Look.
VICTOR	He died contented...
PUGACHEV	Looks as if he's fallen asleep reading...
VICTOR	Pray it's that way for us, comrade — such peace! Such calm. To sleep, aye, perchance to read a paper. And sink, without care to shake this weary coil — the dead rest in peace.
PUGACHEV	Rigor mortis — let's go *Exits*

VICTOR   *Following* Butcher you have no imagination. How you exist is beyond me. *Exits*
Semyon opens his eyes and stares at coffin. During following speech he opens coffin, begins to arrange pillow and smooth cloth; during speech the sound of clock ticking grows gradually louder

SEMYON   I have no imagination, I'm a failure in every way — why haven't scientists figured out a way that a person can commit suicide without feeling it? Like committing suicide under chloroform; and they claim to be humane! Sons of bitches, no imagination either...
He prays over coffin
Dear God, give me the strength to kill myself. Without you I am nothing, without you I am alone, a fragment, insignificant...
He closes his eyes, the gun starts to rise slowly
...a worm, less than a worm, a cockroach, a mosquito, a gnat, a flea, a squashed flea, Dear Lord give a squashed flea the strength to be a speck of blood on your fingernail...
Opens his eyes, goes to clock and stops pendulum, puts gun to his head
...Now.
Masha and Serafima run in

SERAFIMA   They're coming!

MASHA   I couldn't get him alone!

SEMYON   Who?

SERAFIMA   Everyone!

MASHA   *Rushes into kitchen* God help us!

SEMYON   Don't waste your breath. *Sound gets closer*

SERAFIMA   *Following Masha* Masha!

SEMYON   Hide! *Looking for a place to hide* The foxes have their holes, the birds their boughs, but me... *Jumps in coffin*
The door bursts open. Enter Aristarkh, Alexander, Margarita, Victor, Pugachev, Cleopatra, Raisa, Old Woman, Yegor, a Deacon. Re-enter Masha and Serafima. They stretch out their arms in panic and try to hold back the crowd. Many carry flowers... crowd talks and moves about freely

MASHA   Try to see it from his point of view!

SERAFIMA   Some people don't like to die!

MASHA   And who's to blame for that?!

ARISTARKH   Others are to blame, Masha.

SERAFIMA   No one's blaming you, dear friends!

MASHA   What are you going to do to us?!

ARISTARKH   We'll replace your husband in a collective effort.

MASHA	But he's alive! He'll prove it. Semyon? *Sees coffin* Semyon!
ARISTARKH	A chair for the widow.
SERAFIMA	Masha? *Sees coffin* Holy Mother!
MASHA	What's happening?
ARISTARKH	Two chairs!
	Some move to help Masha and Serafima — others gather at coffin — others rearrange wreaths and furniture
MARGARITA	He looks dignified.
CLEOPATRA	Like he were alive.
RAISA	Only his nose is a little pointier.
ARISTARKH	*To Alexander* Tell the Deacon to begin as soon as he can.
MASHA	He's alive! He's alive!
RAISA	Poor woman.
MARGARITA	Affected her head.
ALEXANDER	Calm down, my dear.
SERAFIMA	*Runs to coffin* He's alive!
YEGOR	Watch the old one.
SERAFIMA	Wake up! Wake up!
YEGOR	*Grabbing her* Stop. Stop.
CLEOPATRA	How they're suffering.
ALEXANDER	That happens in the beginning.
MASHA	Why won't you believe me?
SERAFIMA	*Doing battle* Take your hands off me!
ALEXANDER	For nights I couldn't sleep.
ARISTARKH	Alexander Petrovich!
ALEXANDER	*Going to Aristarkh* Ask Margarita.
MARGARITA	*To Deacon* Let's sing something easy.
RAISA	Something we all know.
CLEOPATRA	How they're suffering.
MASHA	He's alive, I know it.
SERAFIMA	Masha! The bastards!
	Masha and Serafima embrace and huddle together. Yegor tries to comfort them. Raisa, Cleopatra, Margarita form a choir under Deacon's guidance. Alexander, Aristarkh pursue business. The choir and Deacon sing a hymn. Pugachev stands over coffin alone. Hymn singing begins
ARISTARKH	*To Alexander* Have you made copies of the suicide note?
ALEXANDER	My secretary's working on it.
YEGOR	Death itself has no meaning.
ARISTARKH	And the money?
ALEXANDER	Not yet.
ARISTARKH	Do it now. *Alexander goes to Pugachev*
YEGOR	Comrade Stalin has proven that.
VICTOR	*To Aristarkh* Tomorrow the papers will have poor Podsekalnikov.

ARISTARKH	No use thinking like that.
YEGOR	Then you mustn't think of that.
ARISTARKH	We're not interested in the deceased as such, we're interested in his service to us.
VICTOR	And how to serve him up.
ALEXANDER	*To Pugachev* When do you plan to settle our account?
VICTOR	That's all I meant.
YEGOR	But the reason for dying, that inspires!
ALEXANDER	The man's on the table, that means cash on the line.
VICTOR	You should understand that.
YEGOR	You should have seen him near the end.
VICTOR	The deceased is not altogether outstanding, thus we emphasize how common he is, his pathos.
ALEXANDER	The business world has a responsibility here.
VICTOR	And win sympathy with familiarity.
YEGOR	One phone call.
ARISTARKH	It would have been much better if a more socially responsible figure...
ALEXANDER	Have you money?
ARISTARKH	Like Gorky, for instance...
VICTOR	That's true.
SEMYON	That's very true!
ALEXANDER	Don't split hairs.
ARISTARKH	Or a government official had committed suicide.
VICTOR	They will, eventually.
SEMYON	I don't agree.
ALEXANDER	You have money.
VICTOR	But we must go step by step.
ALEXANDER	What then?
VICTOR	Fedya Petunin.
ARISTARKH	Who?
ALEXANDER	Good man. *Leaves Pugachev*
VICTOR	Our logical next step.
	Choir finishes. Deaf Mute has wandered in
MARGARITA	Don't be shy. Come in.
SEMYON	Masha!
MARGARITA	You want to see the body?
	Deaf Mute stands at coffin, lights candle, prays. The choir echoes the Deacon in recitative
DEACON	Bless our Sovereign Lord. *Choir*
ALEXANDER	*To Aristarkh* All settled.
ARISTARKH	Speed this business up.
MASHA	No! No! I'll never believe it. Never.
SERAFIMA	Masha, it's no use.
DEACON	In His holy word... *Choir*

59

ALEXANDER	The word of God is indeed holy, but considering the audience, shorten it.
DEACON	Shorten it. *Choir*
ALEXANDER	Now.
	Choir mistakenly picks this up. Deacon begins to rush, a chaotic flow, followed by choir
SERAFIMA	It's fate, Masha.
DEACON	Lord have mercy... *etc.*
MASHA	*Rushes to coffin, pulls at Semyon* Semyon, wake up!
SERAFIMA	He's dead, Masha.
PUGACHEV	Stop!
VICTOR	Sacrilege.
SERAFIMA	He did it finally.
MASHA	No!!!
VOICES	She's fainted. She's dead. Heart attack.
	Choir moves to Masha. Semyon sits up in coffin, with handkerchief, drying his tears
SEMYON	Masha!
	Deaf Mute sees Semyon, shrieks and falls flat on his back
VOICES	What happened? Another?!
ARISTARKH	Get the coffin out of here, quickly. Everyone! Out!
VOICES	Is it spreading? What is? A virus!
ARISTARKH	We'll lay him in state for three days in the chapel where the people can see him.
MASHA	Where...? Am I alive?
SERAFIMA	I'll get you some water.
	Serafima exits into kitchen. Crowd exiting with great noise and confusion. Deaf Mute approaches Masha wildly, in his horror takes out handkerchief and tries to mime what he saw
MASHA	He's dead... I know... stop, you'll hurt yourself! He's dead, I know...
	She calms Deaf Mute, who is still miming with handkerchief. Crowd and noises in distance now
	Don't cry, you feel sorry, I know... if only you knew how sorry I feel... don't cry.
	Embraces Deaf Mute

END OF ACT IV

the SUICIDE

ACT V

ACT V	*Graveyard. A mound of earth beside a freshly dug grave. In shadow near grave stands Cleopatra, and an old woman kneeling. To one side, Alexander, Aristarkh and Victor.*
ALEXANDER	Over here, comrades, look at it from here — how do you like it?
ARISTARKH	A good location.
ALEXANDER	Picked it out myself.
VICTOR	We must say Podsekalnikov picked it out.
ALEXANDER	Why?
VICTOR	So that his life may appear all of a piece — he chose to lie here where once he fought for the revolution.
OLD WOMAN	Lying in the chapel for two days he was.
VICTOR	Or something like that.
ALEXANDER	What are you talking about?
OLD WOMAN	Poor Podsekalnikov.
ARISTARKH	Create a myth.
VICTOR	Or say he used to walk here to formulate his ideas...
OLD WOMAN	They say he took his own life.
VICTOR	Anything poignant and sincere from his past.
ARISTARKH	I agree — good man.
OLD WOMAN	Why? Why?
VICTOR	All that's important is that his life was a simple act of faith, uncluttered by doubt, his sense of purpose guiding him straight as an arrow!
OLD WOMAN	It's obvious...
ARISTARKH	To his destiny.
OLD WOMAN	So obvious — what a hard life!
ARISTARKH	You see, Alexander Petrovich, what's important now is to influence public opinion.
ALEXANDER	Oh, I see that.
OLD WOMAN	If I wasn't so old I'd throw a rope over a tree...
ALEXANDER	But what will his friends say?
OLD WOMAN	And hang myself.
ARISTARKH	Unimportant — the truth will bury them.
VICTOR	We must stir up the people's interest, no matter what.
OLD WOMAN	This graveyard's not interesting any more.
ARISTARKH	Hard at the best of times.
OLD WOMAN	I go to every funeral — boring.
VICTOR	People have grown so selfish.
OLD WOMAN	Taking a walk here now is boring.
VICTOR	All they think about is themselves; we must construct a truth in which they will recognize themselves...

ARISTARKH	Disgusting, but the only way to spark them.
OLD WOMAN	These days the dead are firewood, they burn them.
VICTOR	It's the only way.
ALEXANDER	Whatever you say.
OLD WOMAN	And when I look at the tombstone, oh dear...
ALEXANDER	Here's the bill for the plot.
OLD WOMAN	I know there's no one lying under it only a bottle with some ashes.
ARISTARKH	Is the rest of the funeral arranged?
ALEXANDER	Yes.
ARISTARKH	Everything under control?
ALEXANDER	As you wish.
VICTOR	Fedya Petunin.
ALEXANDER	What?
VICTOR	Was he invited?
ARISTARKH	Were all the invitations sent out?
ALEXANDER	Yes, all of them.
VICTOR	You're sure?
OLD WOMAN	They're not thinking about the future.
ALEXANDER	I'm sure.
OLD WOMAN	That's why they burn them.
ARISTARKH	You can check, Victor Victorovich.
VICTOR	He is our future.
OLD WOMAN	And when the Resurrection day comes there'll be no one to resurrect.
ARISTARKH	Let's get started. *They begin to go*
OLD WOMAN	Oh dear, dear...
VICTOR	Next time a public confession, not just a note.
CLEOPATRA	I must confess!
ARISTARKH	Good idea.
OLD WOMAN	Dear, dear...
VICTOR	It's more artistic.
CLEOPATRA	I killed him. I couldn't help myself.
ALEXANDER	I don't agree — get it in writing.
CLEOPATRA	Podsekalnikov! I made you suffer and now I must suffer.
OLD WOMAN	Dear, dear...
VICTOR	Leave it to us artists, will you?
CLEOPATRA	Forgive me, I shall confess all.
OLD WOMAN	What's done is done. Oh dear...
	Exit Alexander, Aristarkh, Victor
CLEOPATRA	My mother was a gypsy. She was a prisoner of her body and went mad — poor bitch. I'm not ashamed. At fifteen she threw me out. I was beautiful. I remember in Tiflis once I took a cab downtown to buy some shoes and the owner of the store couldn't control himself and bit me on the foot so

badly I had to be taken to the hospital. From that time on I have hated men. When I was sixteen a foreigner fell in love with me, he wanted to dress me always in fancy imported clothes, but I said 'no' and left him, his language bored me. Then a communist began to adore me. My God, how he adored me. He sat me on his knee and said, 'Cleo, mon petit choux, I will open new worlds for you, let's go to Petersburg', but I said 'no' and he cursed me and left the party. Then an airplane pilot fell in love with me, but I just laughed in his face, so he flew over the city crying my name into the air, until he crashed... and now Podsekalnikov. Women fell at his feet, Raisa was in a fit of passion and kept a vigil at his door, but he only wanted me — I was his sun, his moon, his universe — 'without me,' he said, 'I am without light.' He wanted my body, he wanted all of me, but I said 'no', then suddenly bang one afternoon and this humble young man never sees day again. I can't stand it any longer. I loathe my mother. I loathe myself. There is no light in me, only darkness.

Funeral chant begins. Funeral lights appear in distance

And rising now out of my innermost depths this sickness, this revulsion — I'll make a fool of myself at this funeral, I know I will. What do I care! Let all Moscow know. I am low, I am the lowest — no man could ever want this body again. Podsekalnikov has taken it all. *Funeral approaches* Let Raisa and the others have their lesser men. Raisa is a cheat, but I am worse. Raisa puts her feet under the dresser every morning and does stomach exercises. But me? My mother was a gypsy and I grew and bloomed like a mountain ash, without any tricks, and now, and now...

Cleopatra collapses in tears. Funeral procession enters. The Deacon, coffin, Masha, Serafima, Margarita (holding a bowl of 'Kutya', steamed rice with honey eaten on special occasions), Aristarkh, Alexander, Victor, Pugachev, Yegor, Raisa, Old Woman, Boys, etc.

CHOIR	Eternal memory... Eternal memory... *etc.*
ALEXANDER	Coffin there.
SERAFIMA	Don't push the widow!
ALEXANDER	Mourners here, others...
MARGARITA	Careful, careful, you'll spill the rice.
ARISTARKH	Let the first speaker begin.
VICTOR	Yegor's first, representing the masses.
ARISTARKH	You may begin, Yegor.
YEGOR	I'm afraid.
VICTOR	Graveside words are not so frightening.

YEGOR	How can you say that? A word is not a pigeon, once it's out you can't catch it, but then the authorities can catch you and put you in a cage.
ARISTARKH	Yegor Timofeevich.
YEGOR	I refuse. Besides I don't know where to begin.
VICTOR	I have a perfect beginning for you — start it like this — 'Something is rotten in the state of Denmark'.
YEGOR	Who said so?
VICTOR	Marcellus.
YEGOR	Why didn't you say so before? *Runs to mound of earth* Let the speaker through. Stop the singing. *Choir chant stops* Comrades, in these heavy times allow me to share some good news with you. Just a moment ago we received word from Comrade Marcellus that there is something rotten in the State of Denmark. I congratulate all of you, but we should have expected that. The rotten capitalist system has revealed itself. Who's puling at me?
VICTOR	What are you babbling about!?
VOICES	Is it true? Denmark? Wonderful.
VICTOR	That was just something to get you started.
SERAFIMA	We can always count on Yegor for a little relief.
VICTOR	From there you were to move on to the deceased.
YEGOR	The deceased? Of course. Comrades! Not only is something rotten in Denmark, but one of our own has passed away, but dry your tears and march bravely forward in step with the deceased. Now back to Denmark — stop pulling me! Denmark is... *Aristarkh, Alexander and Victor pull Yegor off the mound*
VOICES	What happened? Denmark? What's going on?
ALEXANDER	Dear friends, the previous speaker is not feeling very well — the wound is too fresh, the loss too heavy, he is choked with tears.
MASHA	What's the use of living then, comrades? *Pause*
ARISTARKH	*To Alexander* Say something, idiot.
MARGARITA	Quiet, Masha, you're disturbing the speaker.
SERAFIMA	*Menacing Margarita* Leave her alone!
ALEXANDER	Victor Victorovich?
VICTOR	*Climbing on mound* I will read passages from a poem I have just written for the deceased: No longer mourn for me when I am dead Than you shall hear the surly sullen bell Give warning to the world that I am fled From this vile world with vilest worms to dwell.
RAISA	How delicately put. *She applauds, others join in*

YEGOR	I want to read something too. Let me through.
VOICES	What? Who? Stop him! Help him!
YEGOR	*Jumps on mound* Don't touch me. I am now going to read a poem on Death and its stirring of the masses to action. You, Masha, turn this way and watch my hand. When I move my hand you say 'Who?' like this — *Makes signal* 'Who?' Got it? Are you ready?
VICTOR	Aristarkh Dominikovich?
YEGOR	'Death, and the stirring of the masses.'
ARISTARKH	He'll pay for this.
VOICES	Quiet! Shhh! Shhhh!
YEGOR	*in iambics*
	If he were living in this land
	And serving the great state
	He would be the best foreman — *Makes signal*
SERAFIMA	*Holding Masha who is crying* Who?
YEGOR	Podsekalnikov! Good, eh?
VICTOR	Aristarkh Dominokovich, say something, this is a disgrace.
YEGOR	If he were living in this world
	Still serving the great state,
	He would be the best — *Makes signal*
	Alexander grabs his hand, Yegor flies off the mound. Aristarkh begins immediately
ARISTARKH	Podsekalnikov is no more. I believe his death is the first alarm pointing to the impoverishment of the Russian intelligentsia. But it's only the first — one swallow doesn't make a summer. And I am certain that each one of us, if he dared to look in his own heart, would be forced to admit — Today, Podsekalnikov. Tomorrow...?
CLEOPATRA	*Bursting through crowd to coffin* I confess!
VOICES	Who's that? What? Crazy woman!
CLEOPATRA	I came not to say farewell but to greet you.
VOICES	Mad! Who? Crazy!
CLEOPATRA	You took your life because of me, and I know now what I must do!
SERAFIMA	*Throwing Cleopatra off coffin* Get off my son-in-law!
MASHA	Excuse me, madam, but you've made a mistake — that's my husband.
CLEOPATRA	What does it matter? He wanted my body, he wanted all of me, but I said 'No'.
RAISA	She's lying. I said no, and meant it!
CLEOPATRA	You!
RAISA	He wanted to die for me, but I said forget it.
CLEOPATRA	He died for me!
ARISTARKH	He's not dead! he's alive! Amid mistrust and malevolence

	his example shines with...
VICTOR	If the truth were known.
ALEXANDER	Ladies, he's dead, it's enough.
CLEOPATRA	My body!
RAISA	Your body?
VICTOR	He died for art.
ARISTARKH	*To Victor* Traitor!
PUGACHEV	For business.
CLEOPATRA	For love.
RAISA	Bullshit!
SERAFIMA	*Climbing on mound* Comrades!!! He died for liverwurst.
CLEOPATRA	This is petty jealousy!
MASHA	But will none of you pray for him!?
	Pause
ARISTARKH	*Kneeling at coffin* Podsekalnikov, I alone pray for your resurrection — forgive them, you died for the intelligentsia, forgive them and forgive me — forgive the world, and forgive me. *Kisses Semyon's forehead*
SEMYON	*Embracing Aristarkh* Forgive me too. *Kisses him*
ARISTARKH	Ahhh!!! *Collapses into crowd*
ALL	Help!!!
SEMYON	*Climbing out of coffin* And all you dear people, forgive me!
MASHA	Semyon! Semyon! *Chases him*
SEMYON	*Runs to Margarita* Margarita Ivanovna!
MARGARITA	*With rice in her hands* Keep away from me, Satan! What do you want?
SEMYON	Rice, give me the rice, give it to me! *Gobbles rice* Comrades I must eat...
MASHA	*On her knees embracing Semyon* Semyon!
SEMYON	For two nights and a day I lay in that coffin. I only managed to sneak out of the chapel once to buy a few rolls.
SERAFIMA	*Grabbing bowl* Don't gobble your food!
VOICES	A miracle! Resurrection! What does it mean!?
SEMYON	Hello Masha, it's just me.
ARISTARKH	*Hidden in crowd* Podsekalnikov! — *Emerging* you were to die!
SEMYON	I didn't want to die — not for you, not for them, not for my class, not for humanity, not for Masha...
ARISTARKH	Disgusting!
SEMYON	Not for art, not for business, not for religion, not even for God himself!
VOICES	Blasphemy! Coward! Thank God! Sick!
ARISTARKH	But what about the common good?
CLEOPATRA	What about the individual?
VICTOR	Shoot him!
ARISTARKH	The basis of all society!

VICTOR	We're all exposed now!
SEMYON	I'll tell you what society is!
YEGOR	You're alive? *They shake hands*
SERAFIMA	*Pushing Pugachev* Stand back!
SEMYON	Society's a factory of slogans, and I'm not interested in factories, I'm sorry!
RAISA	We've all been fooled!
VOICES	Coward! Let's get him! Now! Get back! *Pushing*
ALEXANDER	*To Margarita* Which side are we on, my dear?
SEMYON	I'm only interested in living, breathing people! So don't talk to me of 'the common good' or 'the individual' — do you think that when someone screams: 'War! War's been declared!' a man asks what are the issues? Not any more.
VICTOR	For truth!
RAISA	Liar.
CLEOPATRA	Shoot him!
SEMYON	He asks what age group they're enlisting.
CLEOPATRA	All my suffering for nothing?!
SEMYON	There's the truth.
VICTOR	For ideals!
RAISA	Shoot him!
ARISTARKH	Recant, Podsekalnikov, shoot yourself!
YEGOR	Run Semyon!
MASHA	Run!
	Semyon chased. Much shoving and pushing. Ranks form; Masha, Serafima, Yegor defend Semyon. Pugachev is usually caught in the middle
MARGARITA	*To Alexander* I can't decide, you decide, I'm tired.
ALEXANDER	I can't decide.
RAISA	*To Masha* Give me that hat! *They fight*
	Semyon runs to coffin, jumps in, retrieves gun and stands up
SEMYON	*Gun to temple* I will!!!
MASHA	Semyon!
SERAFIMA	Not again.
SEMYON	But I have one thing to say first. Two things... First, I am sorry if what I say is a disappointment to you — I'm a great disappointment, even to myself at times — but as I lay in that coffin, comrades, I thought of all of you — in life you can be my family, my lovers, even my most intimate ones — as you all are! — But in the face of death what can be closer, more loved, more related to one than a hand, a foot, one's stomach — I am in love, comrades, madly in love with my stomach!
VICTOR	You're stalling!
MARGARITA	*To Alexander* Two days in a coffin?

VICTOR	He's stalling!
VOICES	Shoot! No! Shoot! Why?
MARGARITA	And he's in love with his stomach?
ALEXANDER	Hardly profound, is he?
SEMYON	And two!
ARISTARKH	Are you implying there are no heroes in this world?
SEMYON	Comrades, there may be anything in this world — even bearded women! Who am I to say?
PUGACHEV	*Crying* Everything I believed in, crushed!
CLEOPATRA	You are a mockery!
VICTOR	Of truth!
RAISA	Of justice!
ARISTARKH	Of simple human dignity!
VOICES	Let's get him now! Now! *They push forward*
SEMYON	I will!!!
MASHA	Semyon!
SERAFIMA	Make up your mind.
SEMYON	Point two — and this should interest you — I'll return whatever money you spent on me and my family. I'll pay it all back.
RAISA	What is money?!
SEMYON	Every last penny, you'll see — I'll sell my dresser, if I have to comrades, I'll even stop eating! I'll make Masha work for you, I'll send my mother-in-law to the coal mines. I'll even go out and beg! Only let me live!
VOICES	*Much laughing* Coward! He's not worth it! I'd never sink so low! Worm! He's shaking!
SERAFIMA	Bite the hand that feeds him!
VICTOR	What now? After that?
ARISTARKH	Kill him.
VICTOR	Is he worth it?
MARGARITA	*To Alexander* Have you decided?
ALEXANDER	I like him, the makings of an opportunist...
MARGARITA	Like you! *She laughs*
PUGACHEV	*Coming to Semyon, crying* But you said...
SEMYON	I know I said...
PUGACHEV	You would...
SEMYON	I did.
VOICES	Shhh, Shhh, he's talking again.
SEMYON	The thought of death softened my life, my wretched inhuman life — I existed, and suddenly I was out of favour, I was unemployed, and why? Did I ever shirk my responsibility to society? Perhaps I was wrong to take it so personally, but I couldn't help it. I didn't run away from the October Revolution, I didn't go out of the house the whole month, but I didn't run away. I have witnesses to prove it!

70

YEGOR	Disgrace. *He joins Aristarkh and others*
SEMYON	But when the revolution asked, I voted for it, my right hand went up, and now it's voting against me! So keep your achievements, your machines and your crimes, everything, bombs and conquest!
VOICES	*Low muttering* Coward... traitor... yes... no... no.
ALEXANDER	What's this?
SEMYON	All I want is a quiet life and a decent income!
VOICES	What! Disgrace! What does that make us!?
YEGOR	Counter-revolutionary!
VICTOR	The time has come!
ALEXANDER	*To Margarita* Don't like that last bit, no.
SEMYON	I can't help myself!
ALEXANDER	Let's side with the majority.
PUGACHEV	I'll go behind him.
VICTOR	*Directing people* You, over there... *Sound of funeral march has been growing offstage — now heard*
ALEXANDER	What's that. *He exits*
CLEOPATRA	*To Pugachev* Use that shovel!
RAISA	*To Victor* Here's my hat pin!
SERAFIMA	Our great talker!
MASHA	Semyon, I'm afraid. *They circle Semyon, Masha, Serafima*
SEMYON	I can only live as I've always lived — as all of us here have always lived — in whispers. I beg you, don't take that away from me and my family.
ARISTARKH	Have you anything more to say?
SEMYON	Allow us to whisper: 'it's a hard life' — because it makes it easier to live when we can confide in each other how hard it is. I beg you in the name of millions of people, give us the right to whisper: 'it's a hard life'. You won't even hear it there's so much construction of socialism going on. I assure you, we'll live our whole life in a whisper — I beg you.
ARISTARKH	I spit on you! *He does*
SEMYON	Here. *Holding gun out*
ARISTARKH	*Backing, as whole circle does* Put the gun down.
SEMYON	Step forward and take it — if you must.
ARISTARKH	Put it down I said.
SEMYON	Shoot yourself if you must — if I'm guilty of anyone's death, let him step forward and shoot me, if he must. *Sound of funeral march offstage. Alexander runs on*
ALEXANDER	Fedya Petunin has shot himself. He left a note.
ARISTARKH	What does it say?
ALEXANDER	'Podsekalnikov is right, life's not worth living'.

THE END